Yah Chanan the Beloved

The Evangelism of Yah Chanan
(The Gospel of John)
Literally Translated & Transliterated
from
Ancient Aramaic & Hebraic Manuscripts

© 1995 by Herb Jahn
ISBN 0 9631951 5 8

exegeses BIBLES
POBox 1776 • Orange CA • 92668

Phone or Fax
1 800 9 BIBLE 9

TEXTUAL CRITICISM

Student Requisites:	Intense Interest
Classroom:	Wherever
Classtime:	Whenever
Exegete:	Herb Jahn

A manuscript is a manually scribed scribing. The scribings with which we are most concerned are known collectively as Scripture.

Scripture is a series of scribings scribed by scribes — of holy persons moved by the Holy Spirit.

Scripture consists of what humanity has named the Old Covenant and the New Covenant — both of which were originally scribed in the Semitic languages.

The Scribings of the Old Covenant were so carefully copied, that if a scribe made even the slightest error, or spilled a drop of ink, the total manuscript was destroyed.

These scribings had no distinctive upper or lower case letters as we know them, and consisted only of consonants with no vowels. The sounds were carried by tradition from generation to generation. There are rather accurate copies of these scribings in existence to this day.

This accuracy continued until somewhere between the fifth and eighth centuries A.D. At this time the Masorites took it upon themselves to insert vowel and punctuation points, and even added marginal notes. And thus, the first Version of Scripture was produced. Most of the Old Covenant translations of today are translations of this Masoritec Version.

The New Covenant is a much more complex matter. Most of the scribings on which our many versions are based were scribed in Hellene (also known as Bible Greek). And while they claim to be accurate manuscripts, there is great divergency between them.

The most widely accepted version, the Textus Receptus (Received Text) indicates no difference between Lord, LORD, or Yah Veh.

The Nestle Version distinguishes between Lord, LORD, and Yah Veh by inserting the article, the, when Lord is indicated (except in the Evangelism of Loukas).

This is most confusing, as our Lord Yah Shua Meshiach (Jesus Christ) spoke Aramaic and Hebraic. You may confirm this in your Webster's Unabridged Dictionary. This being true, most all today's versions are translations of translations.

Many proofs of the Aramaic and Hebraic are evident even in the Hellenic versions. In all the Evangelisms (Gospels) except Loukas (Luke), one reads the Aramaic and Hebraic words Yah Shua spoke. Paulos the Apostle tells us that he conversed with Yah Veh in Hebraic. And his translation, Maranatha, is Aramaic.

Most fortunately for us, some scribings of the New Covenant in Aramaic and Hebraic have been preserved, and fragments are still being discovered.

Unfortunately, they have not been preserved as well as the Old Covenant Scribings. But our careful research gives us some insight into what the New Covenant relates. For example, most people understand the Hebraic word shalom to mean peace. But its meaning is much more significant. It includes the state of being fully satisfied and satisfied fully. And that includes the state of total contentment to the payment of a debt — as well as the satisfaction of getting even as in betraying.

One of my first "holy hunches" was that when Yah Shua hung on the stake, the words, "It is finished" were the Semitic, "Shalam", the verb of shalom. And I so translated it in the *exeGeses ready research* and *companion BIBLES*.

So when I first discovered the Semitic Translations of the New Covenant, that was the first verse I proofed. And there it was, "Shalam".

Admittedly, there are some problems with the Semitic Manuscripts of what we call the New Covenant. In our translation and transliteration work, we have allowed what we call the Old Covenant renderings to take precedence over the New Covenant.

This may well be a trust building experience. Considering the fallibility of humanity, with all the possiblity of corruption, and the passage of the eons, how mightily the Scripture has been preserved — preserved so well that none need see eternal destruction, but that all may experience eternal life/salvation.

The reasons the Semitic translation and transliteration are so important are many.

Holy Scripture is one Book. Just because humanity divided it into two portions does not make it so. The four century supposed silence between what humanity calls the Old and New Covenants was not a time of neglect or the forgetfulness of God. It was a necessary time span to fulfill the prophecies of Dani El.

Holy Scripture is scribed in the Semitic languages of Aramaic and Hebraic. When you research this, you will see the harmony of total Scripture. You will recognize the Apocalypse as the fulfillment of prophecies of the prophets.

And so, for now, we bring you, Yah Chanan the Beloved. And as Yah Veh grants us strength and length of days, we are preparing the capstone of Scripture in three phases: first, Yah Chanan the Beloved; second, The New Covenant; and third, an Interlinear of the New Covenant — all translated and transliterated from the Semitic languages into our language of English.

Graced — whoever reads.
Even so, come Lord Yah Shua.
And everyone said, Amen.

YAH CHANAN 1

GENESIS OF THE EVANGELISMS: GENEALOGY OF THE WORD

1:1 In the beginning,
the Word having been,
and the Word having been unto God,
and God having been the Word,
2 he having been, in beginning, unto God,
3 all being through him:
and without him,
not even one being became.
4 In him being life/salvation,
and life/salvation
having the light of the sons of humanity,
5 the light enlightens the darkness;
and the darkness overtakes it not.

THE WITNESS OF YAH CHANAN THE BAPTIZER

6 And there being
a son of humanity apostolized by God;
his name, Yah Chanan:
7 he comes to witness
— to witness concerning the Light
so that, through him, all humanity may trust.
8 He, not being the Light,
but witnessing concerning the Light
9 having been for the light of truth
enlightening every human coming into the cosmos.
10 He, being in the cosmos,
and the cosmos, being through his hand,
and the cosmos knows him not:
11 coming to his own,
his own take him not:

THE GOD BIRTH

12 And whoever takes him
he gives sultanship unto being sons of God
— to them who trust in his name:
13 who, neither of blood,
nor of the will of the flesh,
nor of the will of man,
but of God, are birthed.

THE WORD BEING FLESH

14 And the Word, being flesh, rests within;
and we see his glory
— the glory as of the only birthed of the Father
full of charism and truth.
15 Yah Chanan witnesses concerning him,
and pleads, wording,
This is he of whom I word,
He coming after me, being ahead of me;
because he was from the first:
16 and of his fulness we all take
— and charism for charism.

17 Because the torah
was given through the hand of Mosheh;
truth and charism
became through the hand of Yah Shua Meshiach.
18 No human has seen God — not ever:
the only birthed of God
having been in the bosom of the Father,
he declares.

YAH CHANAN THE BAPTIZER INTERROGATED

19 And this is the witness of Yah Chanan
when the Yah Hudiym apostolize
priests and Leviym from Yeru Shalem
to ask him, Who are you?

20 And he professes, and denies not;
but professes, I — I not the Meshiach.

21 And they ask him, So what? Are you Eli Yah?

And he words, Not I.

Are you that prophet?

And he words, Not.

22 And they word to him, Who are you?
— to give word to them who apostolize us.
What word you concerning your soul?

23 He words,
I — a voice pleading in the wilderness,
Straighten the way of Yah Veh,
as Yesha Yah the prophet words.
Yesha Yah 40:3
24 And those apostolized being of the Pharisiym:
25 and they ask him, and word to him,
So why baptize you,
if you be neither the Meshiach
nor Eli Yah nor the prophet?

26 Yah Chanan answers them, wording,
I baptize — I in water;
and one stands among you whom ye know not:
27 he coming after me, being ahead of me,
of whom I am not worthy
to release his leather sandal.

28 These being in Beth Ania crossing Yarden,
where Yah Chanan is baptizing.

THE WORD IS THE LAMB OF GOD

29 The day after,
Yah Chanan sees Yah Shua coming to him,
and words, Behold the Lamb of God,
who bears the sin of the cosmos!
30 This is he concerning whom I word,
After me comes a man, being ahead of me;
because he was from the first:
31 and I knew him not
but to notify Yisra El,
because of this I come baptizing in water.

THE WORD IS THE SON OF GOD

32 And Yah Chanan witnesses, wording,
I saw the Spirit
descending from the heavens as a dove;
and abiding upon him:
33 and I knew him not:
but he who apostolized me to baptize in water,
worded to me,
On whomever you see the Spirit
descending and abiding
baptizes in the Holy Spirit.
34 And I see and witness,
this is the Son of God.

YAH SHUA BEGINS HIS MINISTRY

35 And on another day
Yah Chanan stands, being with two of his disciples;
36 and looking at Yah Shua walking;
he words, Behold the Lamb of God!
37 — and when the two disciples hear him word,
and they go after Yah Shua.

YAH CHANAN 1, 2

38 And Yah Shua turns
and sees them coming after
and words to them, What seek you?

They word to him, Rabbi!
Where have you been?

39 He words to them, Come and see.
— and they go and see where he has been;
and being with him that day
— having been as hour ten.

THE WORD IS THE SON OF GOD

40 And one of those hearing from Yah Chanan
and going after Yah Shua
has been Andreas the brother of Shimon:
41 who first sees Shimon his brother,
and words to him, I found the Meshiach!

42 And he brings him unto Yah Shua,
and Yah Shua looks at him, and words,
You are Shimon the son of Yonah:
you are called Kepha.

43 Another day he wills to go to Galiyl
and finds Philipaus;
and words to him, Come after me.

44 And Philipaus having been from Beth Sayad
the city of Andreas and Shimon:
45 and Philipaus finds Nathan El, and words to him,
Concerning whom Mosheh scribed
in the torah and in the prophets
— we found him
— Yah Shua of Nazareth, the son of Yauseph.

46 And Nathan El words to him,
Is any good possible being from Nazareth?

Philipaus words to him, Come and see.

47 Yah Shua sees Nathan El coming to him,
and words concerning him,
Behold, truly a son of Yisra El, having no deceit!

48 Nathan El words to him, Whence know you me?

Yah Shua words to him,
Ere Philipaus called to you,
when on the fig tree, I saw you.

49 Nathan El answers him, wording,
Rabbi, you are the Son of God!
You are the Sovereign of Yisra El!

50 Yah Shua words to him,
Because I word to you,
I saw you on the fig tree,
trust you?
Greater than these you see.

51 He words to him,
Amen! Amen! I word to you,
From now on you see the heavens opened,
and the angels of God
ascending and descending to the Son of humanity.

THE FIRST SIGN BY YAH SHUA

2:1 And on day three,
there being a banquet in Qanah, a city of Galiyl,
and the mother of Yah Shua being there,
2 and also Yah Shua and his disciples
are called to the banquet.
3 And lacking fermented wine,
the mother of Yah Shua words to him,
They have no fermented wine.

4 Yah Shua words to her,
What — to me and to you, woman?
My day comes not yet.

5 His mother words to the ministers,
Whatever he words to you, work.

6 And there having been six waterpots of stone
placed according to the purifying of the Yah Hudiym
each holding two — two or three rebia.

7 Yah Shua words to them,
Fill the waterpots with water.
— and they fill them.

8 He words to them, Now bail,
and bring to the arch of the feast.
— and they bring.

9 And when the arch of the feast
tastes the water become fermented wine,
and knowing not whence it became
— but the ministers bailing the water know
— they who filled the water:
— the arch of the feast
calls to the groom
10 and words to him,
All humanity first brings the good fermented wine;
and when they intoxicate, the lesser:
and you guarded the good fermented wine until now.

11 This is the first sign
Yah Shua works in Qanah of Galiyl,
and notifies of his glory:
and his disciples trust in him.

YAH SHUA CLEARS THE PRIESTAL PRECINCT

12 After this he descends to Kaphar Nachum
— he and his mother
and his brothers and his disciples
being there few days.
13 And the pasach of the Yah Hudiym being near,
Yah Shua ascends to Yeru Shalem;
14 and finds in the priestal precinct
those who merchandise bulls and sheep and doves
— and the coindealers seated:
15 and he works a whip from rope
and ejects them all from the priestal precinct
with the sheep and the bulls and the coindealers;
and pours their coins
and overturns their tables.

16 And to those merchandising doves, he words,
Take these hence
and work not the house of my Father
a house of merchandise.

17 And his disciples remember it is scribed,
The zeal of your house consumes me.
Psalm 69:9

YAH CHANAN 2, 3

YAH SHUA PROPHESIES HIS DEATH AND RESURRECTION

18 And the Yah Hudiym answer him, wording,
What sign show you us, that you work these?

19 Yah Shua answers, wording,
Raze this nave, and in three days I raise it.

20 The Yah Hudiym word to him,
Forty—six years to build this nave,
and you, raise it in three days?

21 And he words concerning the nave of his flesh:
22 and when he rises from the house of the dead,
his disciples remember this being worded;
and they trust the Scripture
and the word Yah Shua worded.

THE FEAST OF PASACH

23 And Yah Shua, while having been in Yeru Shalem,
in the pasach, in the feast,
many trust in him,
seeing the signs he works:
24 and Yah Shua entrusts not his soul to them
because of knowing all humanity;
25 and not needing humanity
to witness concerning the son of humanity:
for he knows that having been in sons of humanity.

THE SPIRIT BIRTH

3:1 And there having been one man of the Pharisiym
— his name, Niqadimus
— being an arch of the Yah Hudiym:
2 he comes to Yah Shua by night, and words to him,
Rabbi, we know you are apostolized from God,
a doctor:
for no one can work these signs you work
if not with God.

3 Yah Shua answers, wording to him,
Amen! Amen! I word to you,
if a human is not birthed from above,
he is not able see the sovereigndom of God.

4 Niqadimus words to him,
How is a human able to birth when he is old?
Is he able to enter the womb of his mother again
and birth two times?

5 Yah Shua answers, wording,
Amen! Amen! I word to you,
Unless a human is birthed of water and of the Spirit
he is not able to enter the sovereigndom of God.
6 That birthed of flesh is flesh
and that birthed of Spirit is spirit.
7 Marvel not that I word to you,
you need to be birthed from above.
8 The Spirit puffs where he wills
and you hear his voice;
but know not whence it comes and where it goes:
thus is every human birthed of the Spirit.

9 Niqadimus answers, wording to him,
How is this able to be?

10 Yah Shua answers, wording to him,
You, a doctor of Yisra El, and you know these not?
11 Amen! Amen! I word to you,
What we know, we word;
and what we see; we witness:
and our witness, you take not.

12 If I word to you of the earthly, and you trust not,
how, if I word to you of the heavens trust you?
13 And no human ascends to the heavens,
but he who descends from the heavens
— the Son of humanity who has the heavens.

ETERNAL LIFE

14 And exactly as Mosheh exalted
the serpent in the wilderness,
thus the Son of humanity prepares to be exalted:
15 so that all human trusting in him destruct not,
but eternal life/salvation becomes to them.
Yah Chanan 12:30—34
16 For thus God loved the cosmos:
to give his only birthed Son;
that all who trust in him destruct not
but eternal life/salvation becomes to them.
17 For God apostolized not his Son into the cosmos
to judge the cosmos;
but to enliven the cosmos through him.

18 Whoever trusts in him is not judged;
and whoever trusts not is already judged
— because he trusts not
in the name of the only birthed Son of God.
19 And this is the judgment:
light comes into the cosmos,
and the sons of humanity love darkness
more than light
— because their works vilify.

20 For all working hate, hate the light;
and come not to the light
lest their works be rebuked.
21 And whoever works truth comes to the light.

THE FINAL WITNESS OF YAH CHANAN THE BAPTIZER

22 After these,
Yah Shua and his disciples
come to the earth of Yah Hudah;
and being returned with them, baptizing:
23 and Yah Chanan also baptizing
being in Ainon alongside Shalem
because of much water having been there
— coming and being baptized:
24 for Yah Chanan has not yet been fallen
into the guardhouse.

25 And there being a question
from one of the disciples of Yah Chanan
and the Yah Hudiym concerning purifying:
26 and they come to Yah Chanan, wording to him,
Rabbi, he being with you crossing Yarden,
concerning whom you witness,
behold, he baptizes, and all come to him.

27 Yah Chanan answers, wording to them,
The son of humanity is not able,
by his own soul, to take aught,
if not given him to him from the heavens.
28 You — you witnessed that I worded to you,
I be not the Meshiach;
but I am apostolized ahead of him.

29 He having the bride is the groom:
and the friend of the groom
who rises and heeds him,
cheers great cheer
because of the voice of the groom:
so this my cheer, fulfills.

YAH CHANAN 3, 4

30 He needs to greaten; and me to lessen:
31 for he coming from above
is above all:
he of the earth is of the earth,
and speaks of the earth:
he coming from the heavens is above all.
32 And what he see and hears, he witnesses;
and humanity takes not his witness:
33 and whoever takes his witness
seals that God is true.

34 For he whom God apostolizes
words the word of God:
for God gives not the Spirit by measure.

35 The Father loves the Son
and gives all into his hand.
36 Whoever trusts in the Son
has eternal life/salvation:
and whoever is not convinced of the Son
sees not life/salvation;
but the wrath of God abides concerning him.

YAH SHUA GOES TO GALIYL

4:1 And Yah Shua knows
that the Pharisiym hear
he makes and baptizes many more disciples
than Yah Chanan,
2 — though Yah Shua baptizes not
— but his disciples.
3 He forsakes Yah Hudah and goes again to Galiyl.

YAH SHUA AND THE SHAMARAYIM

4 And he works
to come across among the Shamarayim:
5 and comes to a city of the Shamarayim
called Sychar
— alongside the field Yaaqov gave his son Yauseph;
6 and the well of water of Yaaqov being there:
and Yah Shua, being belabored from the way,
sitting on the well, having been about hour six:
7 and a woman of Shamraya comes to fill water.

And Yah Shua words to her, Give me water to drink.
8 — for his disciples had entered the city
to merchandise for nourishment.

9 The woman — a Shamarayim words to him,
How — you, a Yah Hudiy,
ask drink of me, a woman — a Shamarayim?
— for the Yah Hudiym have no use
with the Shamarayim.

10 Yah Shua answers, wording to her,
If you knew the gift being from God,
and who words this to you, Give me a drink;
you had asked of him,
and he had given you living water.

11 The woman words to him,
My Lord, you have no pail and the well is deep:
so whence have you that living water?
12 Are you greater than our father Yaaqov
who gave this well to us
— from which he drank — and his sons, and his flock?

13 Yah Shua answers her, wording,
All drinking of this water thirst again:
14 and all drinking of the water I give
thirst not eternally;
but the water I give
becomes a well of water within
springing to life/salvation eternal.

15 The woman words to him,
My Lord, give me of this water
that I neither thirst again nor come to bail from here.

16 Yah Shua words to her,
Go, call your master, and come here.

17 She words to him, I have no master.

Yah Shua words to her,
Well worded, I have no master:
18 for you had five masters;
and he whom you now have is not your master
— in this you word truly.

19 The woman words to him,
My Lord, I see you are a prophet:
20 our fathers worshipped in this mountain;
you — you word,
Yeru Shalem is the place we need to worship.

21 Yah Shua words to her,
Woman, trust me, the hour comes,
when you neither in this mountain
nor even in Yeru Shalem worship the Father.
22 You worship what you know not;
we worship what we know:
for life/salvation is of the Yah Hudiym.

23 But an hour comes, and now is,
when the true worshippers
worship the Father in spirit and in truth:
for the Father seeks the likes of these worshippers.
24 For God is Spirit:
whoever worships him
needs to worship him in spirit and in truth.

25 The woman words to him,
I know that Meshiach comes
and when he comes, he doctrinates all to us.

26 Yah Shua words to her, I — I word with you.

27 While wording, his disciples come,
and marvel that he is wording with a woman:
and no human words, What seek you?
or, Why word you with her?

28 And the woman forsakes her waterpot
and goes to the city and words to humanity,
29 Come, see a man,
who worded to me all I ever worked!
Is not this the Meshiach?
30 — and all humanity goes from the city
and comes to him.

THE FOOD OF YAH SHUA

31 Between this, his disciples seek of him,
wording to him, Rabbi, eat.

32 And he words to them,
I have food to feed that you know not.

YAH CHANAN 4, 5

33 So the disciples word among another,
Has humanity brought aught to eat to him?

34 Yah Shua words to them,
My food
is to work the will of him who apostolized me
and to shalam his work.
35 Word not, After four months, comes the harvest!
Behold, I word to you,
Lift your eyes, and see the earth;
for they already attained whitening to harvest:
36 and whoever harvests, takes reward;
and gathers fruit to life/salvation eternal:
so that the sporer and the harvester in union
cheer in union.
37 For this is this word of truth,
Another spores, and another harvests.

38 I apostolize you
to harvest whereon you laboured not:
for another labors, and you enter their labors.

39 And many of that city
of the Shamarayim trust in him
because of the word of the woman having witnessed,
He worded to me all that I worked.

YAH SHUA AND THE SHAMARAYIM

40 And when Shamarayim come to him,
they ask him to be with them;
and being with them two days
41 and many trust in him because of his word.

42 And they word to the woman,
Now, not because of your word, we trust in him:
for we hear and know that this is truly the Meshiach
— the Savior of the cosmos.

43 And after two days Yah Shua goes from there,
and goes to Galiyl;
44 for Yah Shua himself witnessed
that a prophet is not honored in his own city:
45 and when he comes to Galiyl,
the Galiliym receive him,
seeing all the signs
he worked at Yeru Shalem at the feast;
for they had also come to the feast.

THE SECOND SIGN OF YAH SHUA

46 And again Yah Shua comes to Qanah of Galiyl
where he worked the water into fermented wine:
and having been at Kaphar Nachum
a servant of one sovereign whose son is infirm
47 hears that Yah Shua comes
from Yah Hudah to Galiyl:
and he goes to him,
and seeks of him to descend and heal his son
being near dying.

48 Yah Shua words to him,
Whenever you see signs and marvels, you trust not.

49 The servant of the sovereign words to him,
My Lord, descend ere my lad die.

50 Yah Shua words to him,
Go — your son is alive!

And the man trusts the word Yah Shua words to him
and goes:

51 and while descending, his servants meet him,
and evangelize to him, wording, Your lad lives.

52 And he enquires of them what season he healed.

And they word to him,
Yesterday in hour seven the fever forsook him.

53 And the father knows it is at the same hour
Yah Shua worded to him, Your son lives!
— and he trusts — he and all his house.

54 This again is sign two that Yah Shua works,
while coming from Yah Hudah to Galiyl.

YAH SHUA HEALS ON THE SHABBATH

5:1 After these,
there being a feast of the Yah Hudiym;
and Yah Shua ascends to Yeru Shalem:
2 and there having been in Yeru Shalem
one place for baptizing,
called in Hebraically, Beth Hesda;
having been five porticos:
3 and many people being cast in these
— infirm, blind, lame, withered;
awaiting the quaking of the water:
4 for time to time an angel descending into the pool
baptizing and quaking the water;
and whoever is descending first
after the quaking of the water
having been healed of all afflictions having been.

5 And having been one,
having been infirm thirty—eight years:
6 when Yah Shua sees him cast,
and knowing he had much time there,
he words to him, Will you to heal?

7 The infirm answers him, wording,
Yes, my Lord, I have no one,
when a human quakes the water,
to cast me into the baptismal:
but while I come,
another descends ahead of me.

8 Yah Shua words to him,
Rise, take your pad, and walk.
9 — and straightway the man heals,
and takes his pad, and walks.

That day being Shabbath
10 and the Yah Hudiym word to him who is healed,
It is Shabbath:
you are not allowed to take your pad.

11 And he answers, wording to them,
He who worked my healing, worded to me,
Take your pad and walk.

12 And they ask him,
to take your pad and walk?

13 And he being healed knows not who:
— for Yah Shua having hid from him
— there having been a vast congregation
in that place.

YAH CHANAN 5, 6

14 After a time
Yah Shua finds him in the priestal precinct,
and words to him,
Behold, your healing:
sin not again
— lest there be somewhat more vilifying than the first.

15 The man goes,
and words to the Yah Hudiym
that Yah Shua healed him:
16 and because of this
the Yah Hudiym persecute Yah Shua,
and seek to slaughter him;
because he works these, being Shabbath.

17 And Yah Shua words to them,
My Father works until now; and I work.

18 And because of this
the Yah Hudiym seek to slaughter him;
not only for having released the Shabbath,
but also concerning God being his Father
— his soul being equal with God.
read: Philippians 2:5—8

19 And answering, Yah Shua words to them,
Amen! Amen! I word to you,
the Son is not able to work aught from his soul,
but what he sees the Father work:
for what the father works,
these also the Son likewise works:
20 for the Father befriends the Son,
and all he shows him, he works:
and shows him more works than these
so that you marvel.
21 For as the Father raises the dead
and enlivens them,
even thus the Son enlivens whom he wills.

22 For the Father judges no human,
but gives all judgment to the Son:
23 so that all humanity honor the Son,
as they honor the Father.
Whoever honors not the Son
honors not the Father who apostolized him.

24 Amen! Amen! I word to you,
Whoever hears my word
and trusts him who apostolized me
has eternal life/salvation
and comes not into judgment;
but departs from death to life/salvation.

25 Amen! Amen! I word to you,
the hour comes — even now be
when the dead hear the voice of the Son of God:
and whoever hears, lives.
26 For as the Father has life/salvation in himself;
thus also he gives the Son
to have life/salvation in himself;
27 and also authorizes him to work judgment
28 because he is the Son of humanity.

THE TWO RESURRECTIONS

Marvel not at this:
an hour comes,
wherein all who are in the tombs hear his voice,
29 and whoever works good,
goes to the resurrection of life/salvation;
and whoever works evil,
to the resurrection of judgment.

30 I am not able, of my own soul, to work aught:
but as I hear, I judge; and my judgment is just:
for I seek not my will
but the will of him who apostolized me.

31 If I witness concerning my own soul,
my witness is not true:
32 another witnesses concerning me;
and I know
the witness he witnesses concerning me is true.

33 You — you apostolized to Yah Chanan;
and he witnesses concerning the truth:
34 and I take no witness from the sons of humanity;
but I word these, that you live.
35 He, being a candle, shining and enlightening:
and you will to flicker for an hour in his light.

36 And I have witness greater than Yah Chanan:
for the works the Father gives me to shalam
— the works I work, witness concerning me
— that the Father apostolized me.
37 And the Father who apostolized me,
witnesses concerning me.

You neither heard his voice — not ever,
nor saw his semblance:
38 nor have you his word abiding within.
because whom he apostolized, you trust not.

39 Examine the Scriptures;
for in them you hope you have eternal life/salvation:
and these witness concerning me.
40 And you will to not come to me
to have eternal life/salvation.

41 I take no glory from humanity.
42 But I know you have no love of God within.

43 I come in the name of my Father,
and you take me not:
whenever another comes in the name of his own soul,
him you take.

44 How are you able to trust
— you who take glory one by one,
and the glory of one God you seek not?

45 Think you that I accuse you before the Father?
you have one accusing you
— Mosheh, in whom you hope:
46 for if you had trusted Mosheh,
you had also trusted me
— for Mosheh scribed concerning me.
47 If you trust not his Scripture,
how trust you my words?

YAH SHUA FEEDS FIVE THOUSAND

6:1 After these
Yah Shua goes crossing the sea of Galiyl of Tiberiyaus:
2 and a vast congregation goes after him,
because they see the signs he works on the infirm:
3 and Yah Shua ascends the mountain;
and sitting there with his disciples,
4 and being near the feast
— the pasach of the Yah Hudiym,
5 and lifting his eyes,
Yah Shua sees a vast congregation coming to him;
and he words to Philipaus,
Where merchandise we bread to feed them?

YAH CHANAN 6

6 — and he words this to test him:
for he knows what he is preparing to work.

7 Philipaus words to him,
Two hundred dinarii of bread is not sufficient for them
when each take little by little one by one.

8 One of his disciples words to him,
— Andreas, the brother of Shimon Kepha,
9 We have here one child
having about five barley breads and two fish:
but what are they for all?

10 And Yah Shua words, Have all humanity repose.
— and there being much herbage in the place,
the men repose — five thousand in number;
11 and Yah Shua takes the breads and eulogizes;
and distributes to those reposing;
and likewise the fish — as much as they will.

12 And when they satiate, he words to his disciples,
Congregate the crumbs that abound
lest aught destructs.
13 — and they congregate and fill twelve baskets
with the crumbs that abound
from them who ate of the five loaves of barley.

14 And these humans,
having seen the sign Yah Shua worked, word,
Truly this is that prophet coming to the cosmos.

15 And Yah Shua,
knowing that they are prepared to come seize him
to make him sovereign,
departs again into a mountain alone — he alone:
16 and being evening,
his disciples descend to the sea
17 and sitting in a sailer,
and come crossing the sea to Kaphar Nachum:
and being darkened,
Yah Shua had not come to them:
18 and the sea being puffed by a great wind, lifts.

YAH SHUA WALKS ON THE SEA

19 So guiding onward
as twenty—five or thirty stadia;
and they see Yah Shua walking on the lake
and approaching the sailer; and they are awestricken.

20 And Yah Shua words to them,
I — I! Awe not!
21 — so they will to take him into the sailer:
and straightway the sailer,
is to the earth where they are going.

22 The day after,
the congregation stands across the sea
and sees no other sailer being there
but that one wherein his disciples ascended;
and that Yah Shua had not gone with his disciples
in the sailer,
23 and other skiffs being come from Tiberiyaus
alongside about the place they ate the breads
where the Lord eulogized:
24 so when the congregation sees
that neither Yah Shua nor his disciples being there,
they also ascend into skiff
and go to Kaphar Nachum seeking Yah Shua:

25 and when they find him crossing the sea,
they word to him, Rabbi, when came you here?

26 Yah Shua answers them, wording,
Amen! Amen! I word to you,
You seek me, not because of seeing the signs,
but of eating the breads and satiating.
27 Work not for the food that destructs;
but for the food that abides to eternal life/salvation
which the Son of humanity gives you:
for God the Father sealed him.

28 They word to him,
What work we to work the works of God?

29 Yah Shua answers, and words to them,
This is the work of God:
to trust in him whom he apostolized.

30 They word to him,
What sign work you, that we see and trust you?
What work you?
31 Our fathers ate manna in the wilderness;
as scribed,
He gave them bread from the heavens to eat.
Nechem Yah 9:5

32 So Yah Shua words to them,
Amen! Amen! I word to you,
Mosheh gave you not that bread
being from the heavens;
but my Father
gave you the bread of truth from the heavens:
33 for the bread of God
is he who descends from the heavens
and gives life/salvation to the cosmos.

34 They word to him, Our Lord,
Give us evermore this bread.

YAH SHUA, THE LIVING BREAD

35 Yah Shua words to them,
I — I the bread of life/salvation:
whoever comes to me famishes not;
and whoever trusts in me thirsts not eternally.
36 But I word to you,
that you also see me, and trust not:
37 all whom the Father gives me, come to me;
and whoever comes to me, I eject not.
38 For I descended from the heavens
— not to work my will
but the will of him who apostolized me.

39 And this is the will of him who apostolized me,
of all whom he gave me, none of them destruct;
but I raise them again at the final day.
40 And this is the will of my father,
that all who see the Son and trust in him
have eternal life/salvation:
and I raise them at the final day.

41 And the Yah Hudiym murmur concerning him,
because he words,
I — I the bread that descended from the heavens.

42 And they word,
Be this not Yah Shua the son of Yauseph,
whose father and mother we know?
So how words he, I descended from the heavens?

YAH CHANAN 6, 7

43 Yah Shua answers them, and words,
Murmur not one with one.
44 Human is not able to come to me
if not the Father who apostolized me draws him:
and I raise him at the final day.
45 For it is scribed in the prophets,
And they all be doctrinated of God.
So all who hear,
and are doctrinated by the Father, come to me.
Yesha Yah 54:13

46 Not being that humanity has seen the Father,
except him who is from God; he has seen the Father.

47 Amen! Amen! I word to you,
Whoever trusts in me has eternal life/salvation.
48 I — I that bread of life/salvation.

49 Your fathers ate manna in the wilderness,
and died.
50 And this is the bread
that descended from the heavens,
for humanity to eat thereof, and not die.

51 I — I the living bread
descending from the heavens:
whenever humanity eats of this bread,
he lives to the eons:
and the bread I give is my flesh,
which I give for the life/salvation of the cosmos.

52 And the Yah Hudiym striving,
How is this one able to give us his flesh to eat?

53 And Yah Shua words to them,
Amen! Amen! I word to you,
If not you eat the flesh of the Son of humanity,
and drink his blood,
you have no life/salvation in you.
54 And whoever eats of my flesh
and drinks of my blood
has eternal life/salvation;
and I raise him at the final day.
55 For my flesh is truly food,
and my blood is truly drink.
56 Whoever eats my flesh and drinks my blood
abides in me; and I in him.

57 As the living Father apostolized me
— and I live because of the Father;
thus whoever eats me, even he lives because of me.

58 This is that bread
descending from the heavens:
not exactly as your fathers eating manna, died:
whoever eats of this bread lives eternally.
59 — He words these in the congregation,
as he doctrinates in Kaphar Nachum.

60 And many of his disciples who hear him, word,
This is a hard word; who is able to hear it?

61 Yah Shua knows in his own soul
that his disciples murmur concerning this,
and he words to them, This offends you?
62 — so what if you see the Son of humanity
ascending where he was formerly?

63 The spirit enlivens; the flesh profits not:
the words I word to you are spirit
and are life/salvation:
64 but there are humans of you who trust not.
— for Yah Shua knew from formerly
who they are who trust not,
and who is to shalam him.

65 And he words to them,
Because of this I word to you,
humanity is not able to come to me,
if not given by my Father.
66 — because of this word
many of his disciples go back,
and walking not with him.

THE WITNESS OF CEPHAS

67 And Yah Shua words to the twelve
Why? Will you also to go?

68 So Shimon Kepha answers him, wording
My Lord, to whom go we?
You have the word of eternal life/salvation:
69 and we trust and know that you are the Meshiach,
the Son of the living God.

70 Yah Shua words to them,
Have I not selected you twelve
— and one of you is a satan?

71 And he words concerning Yah Hudah
the son of Shimon — the urbanite
for being prepared to shalam him,
— one of the twelve.

7:1 After these Yah Shua walks being in Galiyl:
for he wills not walking in Yah Hudah,
because of the Yah Hudiym seeking to slaughter him.

THE TABERNACLE STAKING CELEBRATION — SUKKOTH/BRUSH ARBORS

2 And being near
the feast of tabernacles of the Yah Hudiym,
3 and his brothers word to Yah Shua,
Depart hence, and go to Yah Hudah,
so that your disciples see the works you work.
4 For humanity works not aught secretly,
and wills being known openly.
If you work these, show your own soul to the cosmos.
5 — for not even his brothers trust in him
— Yah Shua.

6 And Yah Shua words to them,
My own time arrives not yet:
but your own time is always prepared.
7 The cosmos is not able to hate you;
and it hates me — because I witness concerning it
that its works vilify.

8 You ascend to this feast:
I ascend not now to this feast
because my time shalams not yet.

9 He words these
and he abides in Galiyl:
10 and when his brothers ascend to the feast,
then he also ascends
— not openly, but as secretly.

YAH CHANAN 7

11 And the Yah Hudiym seek him being at the feast
and word, Where is he?
12 — and there is much murmuring because of him
among the congregation:
for some word, He is good;
another words, Not — not if he deceives the people.
13 — and humanity
speaks not openly concerning him
because of fearing the Yah Hudiym.

14 Already mid day of the feast
Yah Shua ascends to the priestal precinct doctrinating:
15 and the Yah Hudiym marvel, wording,
How knows this one scrolls, when not doctrinated?

16 Yah Shua answers them, wording,
My doctrine is not my own;
but his who apostolized me:
17 whoever wills to work his will,
understands the doctrine
— whether of God,
or whether I word of my own soul.
18 Whoever words of his own thoughts
seeks glory of his own soul:
and whoever
seeks the glory of him who apostolized him,
he is true:
and having no unjustness in his heart.

19 Gave not Mosheh the torah to you?
And yet no human of you guards the torah!
Why seek you to slaughter me?

20 The congregation answers, wording,
You have a demon!
Who seeks to slaughter you?

21 Yah Shua answers wording to them,
I work one work and you all marvel:
22 because of this Mosheh gave you circumcision
— not because of being of Mosheh,
but of the fathers:
and you on Shabbath, circumcise a son of humanity:
23 whenever a son of humanity,
is circumcised on day of Shabbath,
for cause that the torah of Mosheh
not be released concerning me;
murmur you
because I heal a son of humanity on day of Shabbath?

24 Judge not regarding face,
but judge just judgment.

25 And the humans being from Yeru Shalemiym
word,
Is not this he, whom they seek to slaughter?
26 And behold, he words openly
and they word naught to him.
27 But this — we know from whence he is:
and the Meshiach, whenever he comes,
humanity knows not from whence he is.

YAH SHUA DOCTRINATES IN THE PRIESTAL PRECINCT
28 And Yah Shua lifts his voice
when doctrinating in the priestal precinct, wording,
You both know me,
and you know from whence I am;
and I come not from my own soul,
but true is he who apostolized me
— whom you know not:

29 and I know him, for of him, I am;
and he apostolized me.

30 And they seek to hold him:
but no human casts hands concerning him
because of his hour not being yet come.

31 And many of the congregation trust in him
and word, Whenever the Meshiach comes,
works he more signs than these
which this one works?

32 The Pharisiym hear that the congregation
words these concerning him;
and the Rabbipriests apostolize guards to hold him.

33 Yah Shua words to them,
Yet a little time I am with you,
and I go to him who apostolized me.

34 You seek me, and are not able to find me:
and whence I am, you are not able to come.

35 The Yah Hudiym word among their souls,
Where prepares he to go,
that we are not able to find him?
Perhaps to the place of the people he prepares to go
and doctrinate the heathen.

36 What is this word he words,
You seek, and are not able to find me:
and, Where I am, you are not able to come?

THE INVITATION OF YAH SHUA TO TAKE THE HOLY SPIRIT
37 And on the day
— great and final of the feast
Yah Shua rises and shouts, wording,
If a human thirst, come to me and drink:
38 all who trust in me, as the Scripture words,
streams of living water flow from his belly.
39 — and he words this concerning the Spirit
whom those trusting in him are prepared to take:
for the Holy Spirit not yet being given
because of Yah Shua not yet being glorified.

40 And many of the congregation,
hearing this word, are wording,
This truly is the Prophet.

41 Another wording, This is the Meshiach.

Another words, Comes the Meshiach from Galiyl?

42 Words not the Scripture,
From the sperma of David
and from Beth Lechem his own village of David
comes the Meshiach?
Michah 5:2
43 So being, there becomes a division
among the congregation because of him:
44 and some of them having willed to hold him;
but humanity casts not hands concerning him.
45 So the guards come
to the Rabbipriests and Pharisiym,
and the priests word to them,
Why bring you him not?

46 The guards word to them,
Never worded a son of humanity thus
as this man worded.

YAH CHANAN 7, 8

47 The Pharisiym word to them,
Why? Are you also deceived?

48 Why?
Of the humans of the archs or of the Pharisiym
trust they in him?
49 But this people, not knowing the torah,
is cursed.

50 Niqadimus words to them
— being one of them coming to Yah Shua by night,
51 Judges our torah any son of humanity
if not it first hears him and knows what he worked?

52 They answer him, wording, Are you also of Galiyl?
Examine and see! For no prophet rises from Galiyl.

53 And each goes to his own house,
8:1 and Yah Shua goes to the mountain of Olives.

THE ADULTERESS

2 And at dawn he comes again to the priestal precinct
and all the people come to him;
and while being seated he doctrinates them:
3 and the scribes and Pharisiym
bring him a woman taken in adultery.

When they stand her in their midst.
4 they word to him, Doctor,
this woman was taken openly in the deed
— adulterizing:
5 and in the torah of Mosheh
he misvahs us that those as these be stoned:
so what word you?
6 — they word this to test him
— as being to accuse him.

And Yah Shua stoops under, scribing on the ground:
7 and while they continue asking him,
he straightens himself and words to them,
You not having sinned,
cast the first stone concerning her.

8 And again, while stooping,
he scribes about the earth;

9 and while hearing, they go one by one
beginning from the elders:
and the woman is forsaken alone
having been in their midst.

10 And while Yah Shua straightens himself
he words to her — to the woman,
Where are they?
Is humanity not condemning you?

11 And she words, Not humanity, Lord.

And Yah Shua words to her,
Neither condemn I you:
go, and from now, sin not again.

12 And again Yah Shua words with them,
wording, I — I the light of the cosmos:
whoever comes after me, walks not in darkness,
but finds the light of life/salvation.

13 The Pharisiym word to him,
You witness concerning your own soul;
— your witness not being true.

14 Yah Shua answers them and words to them,
Though I witness concerning my own soul,
my witness is true:
because I know from whence I came,
and where I go;
and you know neither from whence I came,
nor where I go.

15 You judge carnally; I judge no human:
16 and whenever I judge,
and my judgment is true:
because I am not alone
— but I and the Father who apostolized me.

17 And also it is scribed in your torah,
The witness of two men is true.
18 I — I witness concerning my own soul:
and the Father who apostolized me
witnesses concerning me.

19 They word to him, Where is your Father?

Yah Shua answers, wording to them,
You know neither me nor my Father:
if you know me,
you also know my Father also.
20 — Yah Shua words these words
in the house of the treasury
while he doctrinates in the priestal precinct;
and no one holds him
for his hour is not yet come.

21 Yah Shua words to them again,
I go my way;
and you seek me; and die in your sins:
and where I go, you are not able to come.

22 The Yah Hudiym word, Why?
Perhaps he slaughters his own soul
— because he words,
Where I go, you are not able to come.

23 And he words to them,
You are from below; I am from above:
you are from this cosmos; I am not from this cosmos:
24 I word to you, that you die in your sins;
for if you trust not that I — I,
you die in your sins.

25 The Yah Hudiym word, Who are you?

Yah Shua words to them,
Even though I begin to word with you
26 I have much
to word and to judge concerning you:
but he who apostolized me is true;
and what I hear from him, I word to the cosmos.
27 — they know not
that he words to them concerning the Father.

TRUTH LIBERATES

28 Then Yah Shua words to them again,
Whenever you exalt the Son of humanity,
then you know that I — I
and that I work not aught of my own soul:
but as my Father doctrinates me, likewise I word:

YAH CHANAN 8, 9

29 and he who apostolized me is with me:
the Father forsakes me not alone;
for I evermore work what pleases him.
30 — while he words these, many trust in him.

31 And Yah Shua words
to the Yah Hudiym who trust in him,
Whenever you abide in my word
you are truly my disciples;
32 and you know the truth
and the truth liberates you.

33 They word to him, We are sperma of Abraham;
and not ever servient to humanity!
How word you, Being sons of liberation?

34 Yah Shua words to them,
Amen! Amen! I word to you,
All who work sin are the servant of sin:
35 and the servant abides not in the house eternally:
but the Son abides eternally:
36 so whenever the Son liberates you,
you truly be sons of liberation.
37 I know you are sperma of Abraham;
but you seek to slaughter me
because my word suffices you not.

38 What I see toward my Father, I word:
and what you see toward your father, you work.

39 They answer him, wording,
Abraham is our father.

Yah Shua words to them,
If you were sons of Abraham,
you had worked the works of Abraham:
40 and now, behold, you seek to slaughter me,
a man who words the truth I heard from God:
this Abraham worked not:
41 you work the works of your father.

They word to him,
We be not of whoredom; we have one Father — God.

42 Yah Shua words to them,
If God be your Father, you had been loving me:
for I have gone from God;
I came being, not of my own soul,
but he apostolized me.
43 Because why know you not my words?
Concerning your not being able to hear my word:
44 — you being of your father the devouring accuser
and the lust of your father you will to work:
who from the beginning slaughtered humanity;
and stands not in the truth
because the truth is not in him.
Whenever he words a lie, he words of his own:
for he is a liar, also the father thereof.

45 And because I word you the truth
you trust me not.
46 Who of you rebukes me concerning sin?
And if I word the truth,
why trust you me not?
47 Whoever be of God,
hears the word of God:
because of this you hear them not;
because of you not being of God.

48 The Yah Hudiym answer, wording to him,
Word we not well,
that you are a Shamarayim, and have a demon?

49 Yah Shua words, I have no demon;
but I honor my Father, and you dishonor me:
50 and I seek not my own glory:
there be one who seeks and judges.

51 Amen! Amen! I word to you,
Whoever guards my word never sees death to eternity.

52 The Yah Hudiym word to him,
Now we know you have a demon:
Abraham is dead — and the prophets;
and you word,
Whoever guards my word,
never tastes death to eternity.
53 Why?
Are you greater than our father Abraham who died?
And the prophets who died?
Whom make you of your own soul?

54 Yah Shua words,
If ever I glorify myself, my glory be naught:
my Father glorifies me
— of whom you word that he is your God:
55 and you know him not; and I know him:
and if ever I word that I know him not,
I become a liar likewise:
but I know him, and guard his word.
56 Abraham your father
had jumped for joy to see my day:
and he saw, and cheered.

YAH SHUA, THE ETERNAL I — I

57 The Yah Hudiym word to him,
Your years be not yet fifty
— and you saw Abraham?

58 Yah Shua words to them,
Amen! Amen! I word to you,
Ere Abraham became, I — I.

59 And they take stones to stone him:
and Yah Shua secretes himself,
and goes from the priestal precinct,
passing among them, and goes.

YAH SHUA HEALS ONE BIRTHED BLIND

9:1 And crossing over,
he sees a man, blind from the womb of his mother:
2 and his disciples ask him, wording,
Rabbi, who sinned, this — or his father,
when he is birthed blind?

3 Yah Shua words,
Neither this man sinned, nor his father:
but that the works of God be seen in him.
4 I need to work the works of him who apostolized me
while it is day:
the night comes when humanity is not able to work.
5 As long as I am in the cosmos,
I am the light of the cosmos.

6 While wording these,
he spits on the earth and thickens clay from the spit;
and he soils the eyes of the blind;

YAH CHANAN 9

7 and words to him,
Go, wash in the pool of Shilucha*.
*Shilucha = Apostolized
— and he goes and washes and comes seeing:

8 And the neighbors
and whoever had formerly seen him begging,
word, Be not this he who sat and begged?

9 Some had been wording, This is he!
And others were wording, No, but he be like him!

And he words, I — I!

10 They word to him,
How were your eyes opened?

11 He answers, wording,
A man named Yah Shua, worked clay,
and soiled my eyes, and worded concerning me,
Go wash in the water of Shilucha.
— and I go and wash and I see.

12 They word to him, Where is he?

He words to them, I know not.

13 They bring him being formerly blind
to the Pharisiym:
14 and having been Shabbath
when Yah Shua worked the clay.

15 And again the Pharisiym ask him how he sees.

He words to them, He placed clay on my eyes
and I washed and see.

16 And a human of the Pharisiym words,
This man be not of God,
because he guards not the Shabbath.

And another words,
How is a man — a sinner able to work this sign?
— and there is a division between them.

17 They word again to the blind,
What word you
concerning him who opened your eyes?

He words, He is a prophet.

18 And the Yah Hudiym trust not concerning him
that being blind, and sees;
until they call to the father of him who sees:
19 and they ask him,
Is this your son, of whom you word,
blind when birthed?
How now sees he?

20 And his father answers them, wording,
We know this is our son;
and that he was birthed blind:
21 but how he now sees,
or who opened his eyes, we know not;
he is of years; ask him:
he speaks for his own soul.

22 — his parents word these words
because of being awed of the Yah Hudiym:
for the Yah Hudiym had already cut*
*as in cutting a covenant
that whenever humanity professes in the Meshiach,
to eject from the congregation.

23 Because of this, his parents word concerning him,
He is of years; ask him.

24 They call the man having been blind, time two
and word to him, Glorify God!
For we know this man is a sinner.

25 He answers, wording, If he is a sinner, I know not:
and one I know, being blind, behold, I see.

26 And they word to him again,
What worked he to you? How opened he your eyes?

27 He answers them, I word to you,
and you hear not:
Why will you to hear it again? Why?
Will you also be his disciples?

28 And they abuse him and word to him,
You are his disciple;
for we are disciples of Mosheh:
29 we know God worded with Mosheh:
as for this, we know not whence he is.

30 The man answers them, wording,
So this is a marvel,
that you know not from whence he is,
and yet he opened my eyes:
31 and we know
that God hears not the voice of sinners:
but whenever any is awed of God and works his will,
he hears.

32 From eternity it was not heard
that anyone opens the eyes of a human birthed blind.
33 If not being from God,
he is not able to work aught.

34 They answer him, wording,
You are all birthed in sins — and you doctrinate us?
— and they eject him outside.

YAH SHUA, THE SON OF GOD

35 Yah Shua hears they ejected him outside;
and he finds him, and words to him,
Trust you in the Son of God?

36 He who was healed answers, wording,
Who is he, my Lord — so that I trust in him?

37 And Yah Shua words to him,
and he who words with you is he.

38 And he words, I trust, my Lord.
— and he falls to worship him.

39 And Yah Shua words,
I come to this cosmos in judgment,
that whoever sees not, sees;
and whoever sees, blindens.

Yah Chanan the Beloved

Now you can, for the first time ever, read the words of Yah Shua Meshiach (Jesus Christ) and the disciples, literally translated & transliterated directly from Aramaic and Hebraic — the language they spoke. Beginning with the very first five verses, note how the accurate wording of the tenses signify that Yah Shua Meshiach existed from eternity past. This literal translation and transliteration not only brings new meaning, it brings true meaning.

Yah Chanan the Beloved
is a true story of joy, of heartbreak, of denial, and of ultimate victory:
— of spiritual relationships interrupted and restored
— of our blessed hope that can metamorphose us
from eternal destruction to eternal salvation.

Yah Chanan the Beloved
more — much more than a greeting card
— a heartfelt expression your beloved will long cherish
— a fitting remembrance for the wise who win souls
— a bold witness for the merchant to indicate your spiritual ethics.

Yah Chanan the Beloved
— a precious foretaste of the New Covenant now in preparation.
For more information, see Centerfold D.

Quantity Prices — each:
1 — 9 $5
10 — 49 $4
50 — 99 $3
100            $2

SUGGESTION:
You may, if you so desire, pull out this centerfold for safe keeping.

Centerfold A

exeGeses
ready research BIBLE

More than ten years research into the Aramaic, Hebraic, and Hellenic words of the Scripture are behind this **exeGeses ready research BIBLE.** Every one of the more than 14,000 words has been thoroughly researched for you — thus minimizing the research you need to do. The **exeGeses ready research BIBLE** with its myriads of exegeses inserted at the points of occurrence transforms the **Authorized King James Version** into a literal translation and transliteration.

exeGeses ready research BIBLE, Black Bonded Leather $40
exeGeses ready research BIBLE, Burgundy Bonded Leather $40
exeGeses ready research BIBLE, Navy Hard Cover $30

---

exeGeses ready research BIBLE:
The King James Text is in plain type:
Text under exegeses is in oblique type:
Text of the exegeses is in bold type.

PSALM 110:
A psalm of David.
1   *The LORD said* **An oracle of Yah Veh** unto my *Lord* **Adonay**,
Sit **Settle** thou at my right *hand*
until I make set thine enemies
thy footstool **the stool of thy feet.**

ISAIAH 42:
8   I *am the LORD* **Yah Veh**: that is my name:
and my *glory* **honour** shall I not give to another,
neither my *praise* **halal** to *graven images* **sculptiles.**

exeGeses companion BIBLE
Based on the myriads of exegeses
in an easy to read,
easy to comprehand format.

PSALM 110:
A Psalm of David.
1   An oracle of Yah Veh to my
Settle at my right until I set yo
the stool of your fee

YESHA YAH 42:
8   I — Yah Veh: that is my
and I give neither my honor t
nor my halal to sculpti

---

exeGeses
parallel BIBLE

The **exeGeses parallel BIBLE** is two Bibles in one. In the left column, the **exeGeses ready research BIBLE** with its myriads of exegeses inserted at the points of occurrence — and in the right column, the **exeGeses companion BIBLE** for inspiration. Viewed side by side, you read for research and for inspiration, knowing that you always have a literal translation and transliteration at hand.

Includes **LEXICON and SUBJECT SUMMARIES**
number coded to Strong's Concordance.
Herb Jahn, exegete: 1964 pages.

exeGeses parallel BIBLE, Black Bonded Leather $70
exeGeses parallel BIBLE, Burgundy Bonded Leather $70

exeGeses
companion BIBLE

The **exeGeses companion BIBLE** has the same myriads of exegeses in an inspirational, easy to read Translation and Transliteration.

From the Hallalu's of the Psalms to the Hallalu's of the Apocalypse your spirit will indeed be inspired.

The **exeGeses companion BIBLE** is a reverential Literal Translation and Transliteration of the Scripture, in a contemporary classic language, exactly following the tenses and active cases of the ancient manuscript.

The exeGeses companion BIBLE is available only within the exeGeses parallel BIBLE & CDRom.

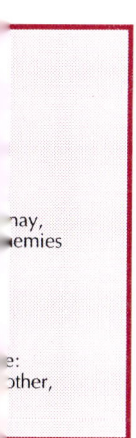

Limited FREE OFFER!
exeGeses parallel BIBLE
FREE with every
exeGeses parallel CDRom

exeGeses
parallel CDRom

Make research even easier! For the ultimate in research tools, use the CDRom and the parallel BIBLE side by side.

Use the CD's search feature to locate specific passages, words, or chapters, and print your selected sections and sermon notes.

A great educational tool for Bible scholars, historians, and language buffs.

Compatible on DOS, Windows, Unix, Macintosh.
exeGeses parallel BIBLE CDRom $80

Centerfold C

Now in Preparation!
the exeGeses New Covenant

literally translated & transliterated
from
Ancient Aramaic & Hebraic Manuscripts

exeGeses BIBLES
is a religious nonprofit corporation chanakkahed to the sole purpose of preparing literal translations & transliterations of Scripture. Even to this day, the exeGeses ready research BIBLE and the exeGeses parallel BIBLE are the only literal translations and transliterations of the Scripture in existence.

They are based on the most reliable Aramaic, Hebraic, and Hellenic (Greek) manuscripts.

Here's what this means to you:
In this day of "watered—down" translations, some even claiming to be "literal", you will now be able to hold in your hand, for the very first time, the most literal translation and transliteration of the New Covenant — translated directly from Aramaic and Hebraic Manuscripts — directly from manuscripts of the language in which Yah Shua Meshiach (Jesus Christ) and the apostles and disciples spoke.

Because these are indentical to the languages of the Old Covenant, you will see for yourself the relationship between the Old Covenant and the New Covenant. In fact you will see for yourself that what humanity has named the Old Covenant and New Covenant are but One Covenant, with a time span between, necessitated in order to fulfill the prophecies of Dani El.

Yah Chanan the Beloved is but a foretaste of the **exeGeses** New Covenant now in preparation.

If you desire to be apprised the moment this precious book is available, send your name and address with the words, "New Covenant" to:
exeGeses BIBLES • POBox 1776 • Orange CA • 92668

Centerfold D

YAH CHANAN 9, 10

40 And some of the Pharisiym being with him
hear this and word to him,
Are we also blind?

41 Yah Shua words to them,
If you had been blind, you had no sin:
and now you word, We see!
because of this your sin abides.

YAH SHUA, THE GOOD SHEPHERD

10:1 Amen! Amen! I word to you,
Whoever enters not by the portal
of the sheepfold of the flock,
but ascends from another place,
is a thief and a robber;
2 and whoever enters by the portal
is the shepherd of the flock:
3 the guard of the portal opens the portal to him
and the flock hear his voice:
and he calls his own sheep by name
and defends them:
4 and whenever he defends his own flock
he goes ahead of them;
and his own sheep go after him;
because they know his voice:
5 and the flock goes not after an alien,
but flees from him:
for they know not the voice of an alien.
6 — Yah Shua words this parable to them
and they know not what he words with them.

YAH SHUA, THE PORTAL

7 And Yah Shua words to them again,
Amen! Amen! I word, to you,
I — I the portal of the flock.
8 All who come are thieves and robbers:
but the flock hear them not.
9 I — I the portal:
whenever anyone enters by me, he is enlivened;
and enters and exits, and is able to find pasture.
10 The thief comes not, if not to thieve
and to sacrifice and to destroy:
I come that they have life/salvation,
and that they have more.

THE GOOD SHEPHERD PLACES HIS SOUL

11 I — I the good shepherd;
the good shepherd places his soul for the flock:
12 and a hireling, not being a shepherd,
whose own the sheep are not,
sees the wolf coming;
and forsakes the flock, and flees:
and the wolf seizes them, and disperses the flock.
13 And the hireling flees, because he is a hireling,
and cares not concerning the flock.

14 I — I the good shepherd and know my own;
and my own flock knows me.
15 As the Father knows me,
I know the Father:
and I place my soul for the flock.

OTHER SHEEP, ANOTHER SHEEPFOLD:
ONE SHEPHERDDOM, ONE SHEPHERD

16 And I also, having other sheep,
not being of this sheepfold:
I need also bring them;
and they hear my voice;
and they each be one flock
and one shepherd.

17 Because of this my Father befriends me,
— I place my soul to take it again:
18 humanity takes it not from me;
but I place it of my own will:
for I have authority to place,
and I have authority to take again:
I took this misvah from my Father.

19 And again, there becomes a division
among the Yah Hudiym because of these words:
20 and many of them word,
He has a demon, and in maddening, maddens!
Why hear him?

21 And another words,
These are not the words of one demonized:
Is a demon able to open the eyes of the blind?

YAH SHUA, THE MESHIACH

22 And being the feast of hanukkah at Yeru Shalem
and being the downpour:
23 and being that Yah Shua walks
in the priestal precinct
in the portico of Shelomoh:
24 and the Yah Hudiym surrounding him,
and wording to him,
Until when take you our soul?
If you are the Meshiach, word to us openly.

YAH SHUA AND FATHER ARE ONE

25 Yah Shua answers and words to them,
I word to you, and you trust not:
the works I work in the name of my Father
witness concerning me:
26 but you trust not,
because of not being of my sheep,
as I worded to you.
27 My sheep hear my voice and I know them;
and they come after me:
28 and I give them eternal life/salvation;
and they destruct not eternally,
nor anyone seize them from my hand.

29 My Father who gave them to me,
is greater than all;
and humanity is not able
to seize them.from the hand of my Father
30 I and my Father are one.

YAH SHUA ACCUSED OF BLASPHEMY

31 And again
the Yah Hudiym take stones to stone him.

32 Yah Shua words to them,
I show you many good works from my Father;
because of which work stone you me?

33 The Yah Hudiym word to him,
For a beautiful work we stone you not;
but because of your blasphemy;
and because you, being a son of humanity,
make your own soul God.
Philippians 2:5—8

34 Yah Shua words to them,
Is not being thus scribed in your torah,
I word, You are gods?
Psalm 82:6

35 If he words them gods,
because to them be the word of God
— and not being able to release the Scripture,

YAH CHANAN 10, 11

36 to him whom the Father hallowed
and apostolized into the cosmos,
You — word you, You blaspheme!
— concerning my word, I — I the Son of God?

37 If I work not the works of my Father,
trust me not:
38 and if I work, though you trust me not,
trust the works:
so that you know and trust,
my Father in me, and I in my Father.

39 And again seeking to hold him;
and he escapes from between their hand
40 and goes again crossing Yarden
to the place
being where Yah Chanan had formerly baptized;
and there he abides.

41 And many sons of humanity come to him,
and having worded,
Indeed, Yah Chanan worked not one sign:
and all Yah Chanan words concerning this man is true.
42 — and many trust in him.

EL AZAR DIES

11:1 And one having been infirm,
El Azar of Beth Ania,
of the village of Maryam and her sister Martha:
2 — that Maryam who anointed with ointment
the feet of Yah Shua
and wiped with her hair
whose brother El Azar having been infirm.
3 And his two sisters apostolize to Yah Shua,
wording, Our Lord,
behold, he whom you befriend is infirm.

4 And Yah Shua words,
This infirmity be not of death;
but for the glory of God
and glorifies the Son of God because of it.

5 And Yah Shua having loved Martha
and Maryam and El Azar,
6 when he hears he is infirm:
he abides in the place where he has been two days:
7 afterwards he words to his disciples,
Come, we go again to Yah Hudah.

8 His disciples word to him, Rabbi,
the Yah Hudiym now seek to be stoning you
— and go you there again?

9 Yah Shua words,
Has the day not twelve hours?
Whenever humanity walks in the day,
he stumbles not,
because he sees the light of this cosmos:
10 and whenever humanity walks in the night,
he stumbles,
because of not having light within.

11 Yah Shua words these:
and afterwards he words to them,
Our friend El Azar sleeps; but I go waken him.

12 His disciples word to him,
Our Lord, if he sleeps, he is healed.
13 — and Yah Shua words concerning his death:
but they hope he words concerning sleep in slumber.

14 Then Yah Shua words to them clearly,
El Azar died:
15 and because of you,
I cheer because I was not there
— so that you trust; but let us walk there.

16 Taoma words, who is worded Twin,
to his companion disciples,
We also go, to die with him.

17 And Yah Shua comes to Beth Ania,
and finds him
having laid in the house of the tomb four days.

18 And Beth Ania having been alongside Yeru Shalem
— apart as by fifteen stadia:
19 and many of the Yah Hudiym
have come to Martha and Maryam,
to fulfill their heart because of their brother.

20 And Martha,
when she hears Yah Shua comes,
goes to meet him:
and Maryam being seated in the house.

21 And Martha words to Yah Shua, Lord,
if you had been here, my brother had not died:
22 but even now, I know,
— as much as you ask of God,
he gives you.

23 Yah Shua words to her, Your brother rises.

24 Martha words to him,
I know he rises in the resurrection at the final day.

YAH SHUA, THE RESURRECTION AND THE LIFE/SALVATION

25 Yah Shua words to her,
I — I the resurrection and the life/salvation:
whoever trusts in me,
even though he dies, he enlivens:
26 and all who live and trust in me
die not eternally.
Trust you this?

27 She words to him, Yes, my Lord:
I trust that you are the Meshiach
— the Son of God coming to the cosmos.

28 And when wording these, she goes,
and calls Maryam her sister covertly,
wording, Our Rabbi has come and calls to you.

29 And Maryam, when she hears
rises quickly and comes to him:
30 and Yah Shua has not yet come to the village,
but being in the place Martha met him.

31 And also the Yah Hudiym
having been with her in the house
who are being comforting to her,
seeing Maryam rise quickly and go,
they go after her;
— for they hope she goes to the tomb to weep.

32 And Maryam,
when she comes to where Yah Shua has been,
and sees him,
she falls about his feet, wording to him,
My Lord, if you had been here,
my brother had not died.

YAH CHANAN 11, 12

33 And when Yah Shua sees her weeping,
and the Yah Hudiym coming with her also weeping,
he sighs in spirit, and his soul quakes:
34 and words, Where have you placed him?

They word to him, Our Lord, come and see.

35 And the tears of Yah Shua come.
36 and the Yah Hudiym word,
See how much he befriends him!

37 And some of humanity word,
Is this one not being able,
— who opens the eyes of the blind,
also work that this one not die?

38 And Yah Shua, sighing within himself,
comes to the house of the tomb
— the house of the tomb having been a grotto;
and a stone having been placed about the portal.

39 Yah Shua words, Take this stone.

Martha, the sister of him who died, words to him,
— for it is four days.

40 Yah Shua words to her,
Worded I not to you,
Whenever you trust, you see the glory of God?

41 And they take the stone
and Yah Shua lifts his eyes about, and words,
Father, I thank you that you hear me:
42 and I know that you hear me evermore:
but I word this because of this congregation standing
— that they trust that you apostolized me.

43 And when he words this,
he shouts with a high voice,
El Azar, come outside!

44 And the dead comes,
hands and feet bound with swathes:
and his face bound with a sudarium.

Yah Shua words to them,
Release him, and let him go.

45 And many of the Yah Hudiym coming to Maryam
when they see what Yah Shua worked, trust in him:
46 and some of humanity
go their ways to the Pharisiym,
and word to them what Yah Shua worked.

47 And the Rabbipriests and the Pharisiym congregate
and word,
What work we? For this human works many signs.
48 Whenever we thus allow him,
all humanity trusts in him:
and the Romans come and take
both our place and our people.

49 And one of them named Qauapha,
being the Rabbipriest that same year,
words to them, You neither know aught;
50 nor reason that it is benefical for us
that one man die in the stead of the people;
that all the people not destruct.

51 — and he words this not from his own soul:
but because of being Rabbipriest that year
he prophesies of Yah Shua being prepared to die
in the stead of the people;
52 and not only in the stead of the people,
but also that the sons of God that are dispersed
congregate as one.

53 And from that day
they reason together to slaughter him:
54 and Yah Shua walks openly no more
among the Yah Hudiym;
but goes to a place near the desolation
— to a city called Ephrayim;
and returns there being with his disciples.

55 And the pasach of the Yah Hudiym being near:
and many ascending
from the villages to Yeru Shalem
preceding the feast to purify their souls.
56 and seeking for Yah Shua;
and wording one to one
in the priestal precinct,
What hope you,— that he comes not to the feast?

57 And the Rabbipriests and the Pharisiym
having misvahed,
that whenever humanity knows where he is,
that he expose it, so as to hold him.

MARYAM ANOINTS YAH SHUA

12:1 And Yah Shua, six days preceding the pasach
goes to Beth Ania where El Azar had been
whom he, Yah Shua,
raised from the house of the dead:
2 and they work him a supper there
and Martha ministering:
and El Azar is one reposing with him.

3 And Maryam takes an alabaster of ointment of nard
— choicest of vast price
and anoints the feet of Yah Shua
and wipes his feet with her hair:
and the house fills from the fragrance of the ointment.

4 And Yah Hudah the urbanite
one of his disciples,
preparing to shalam him, words,
5 Why was not this ointment merchandised
for three hundred dinarii and given to the poor?
6 — and he words this,
not because of being concerned caring for the poor;
but because of being a thief and having the bag
and bearing what falls therein.

7 And Yah Shua words, Allow her:
she guards this to the day of my entombment:
8 for you have the poor with you evermore;
but me you have not evermore.

9 And many of the congregation of the Yah Hudiym
hear that Yah Shua is there:
and they come, not because of Yah Shua only
but to see El Azar
whom he raised from the house of the dead:
10 and the Rabbipriests think
to also slaughter El Azar;
11 because many of the Yah Hudiym,
because of him, going and trusting in Yah Shua.

YAH CHANAN 12

THE TRIUMPHAL ENTRY OF YAH SHUA
12 And on another day,
a vast congregation coming to the feast,
when they hear of Yah Shua coming to Yeru Shalem,
13 they take branches of phoinix and go meet him,
and shouting, and wording, Hoshia Na!
Eulogized — he coming in the name of Yah Veh
— the Sovereign of Yisra El.

14 And Yah Shua finds a burrito and sits thereon;
as scribed,
15 Awe not, daughter of Sihyun!
Behold, your Sovereign comes to you,
mounted on a colt, the son of a burro.
Psalm 118:25, 26; Zechar Yah 9:9

16 His disciples knew these not at the time:
but when Yah Shua was glorified
they remember these being scribed concerning him;
and that they had worked these to him.
17 And the congregation with him witnessing
that he called El Azar from his tomb
and raised him from the house of the dead,
18 because of this a vast congregation goes to him.

19 And the Pharisiym wording one by one,
See you that you gain not aught?
Behold, all the cosmos goes after him!

HELLENES WILL TO SEE YAH SHUA
20 And there having been of the people
— sons of humanity among them
ascending to worship at the feast:
21 they come approaching to Philipaus
who is of BethSayad of Galiyl,
and ask him, wording to him,
My lord, we will to see Yah Shua.

22 Philipaus comes and words to Andreas:
and Andreas and Philipaus word to Yah Shua.

YAH SHUA PROPHESIES HIS DEATH AND GLORIFICATION
23 And Yah Shua answers them, wording to them,
The hour is come
for the Son of humanity to be glorified.

24 Amen! Amen! I word to you,
A grain of wheat,
If not it falls and dies to the earth,
it abides alone:
and whenever it dies, it brings much fruit.

25 Whoever befriends his soul, destroys it;
and whoever hates his soul eternally,
guards it to life/salvation eternal:
26 whenever humanity ministers to me,
they come after me;
and wherever I am, there also be my minister:
whoever ministers to me, my Father honors.
27 Behold, now my soul troubles;
And what word I?
Father, deliver me from this hour?
But because of this, I come to this hour.
28 Father, glorify your name.

And a voice is heard from the heavens,
I glorified, and I glorify again.

29 And the congregation standing by, hear;
and they word of thundering:
another words, An angel words with him.

30 Yah Shua answers, wording to them,
This voice became not because of me;
but became because of you.

THE ARCH OF THE COSMOS CAST OUTSIDE: YAH SHUA EXALTED
31 Now is the judgment of this cosmos;
now is the arch of this cosmos cast outside:
32 and I, whenever I am exalted from the earth,
draw all humanity to me.
33 — he words this, showing what death he dies.
Loukas 10:18, Revelation 12:7—12

34 The congregation words to him,
We hear from the torah
that the Meshiach abides eternally:
and how word you,
The Son of humanity prepares to be exalted?
Who is this Son of humanity?

35 Yah Shua words to them,
Yet a little time the light is with you:
walk while you have the light
that darkness not overtake you:
whoever walks in darkness
knows not where he goes.
36 While you have light, trust in the light
that you be sons of light.

Yah Shua words these
and goes and secretes himself from them:
37 and when he works all these signs
in front of them
they trust not in him:
38 to fulfill the word of Yesha Yah the prophet
who words,
My Lord, who trusts our rumor?
And to whom is the arm of Yah Veh exposed?
Yesha Yah 53:1

39 Because of this they are not able to trust,
because Yesha Yah words again,
40 They blind their eyes,
and darken their heart;
that they not see with their eyes
and understand with their heart
and return, and I heal them.

41 Yesha Yah worded these when he saw his glory,
and spoke concerning him.
Yesha Yah 6:10

42 And also many of the archs trust in him;
but because of the Pharisiym, they profess him not,
that they not be outside of the congregation:
43 for they befriend the glory of the sons of humanity
more than the glory of God.

44 And Yah Shua shouts and words,
Whoever trusts in me,
trusts not in me,
but in him who apostolized me:
45 and whoever sees me,
sees him who apostolized me.
46 I come — a light to the cosmos;
that all who trust in me abide not in darkness:
47 and whoever hears my word
and guards them not,
I judge him not:
for I come not to judge the cosmos
but to enliven the cosmos.

YAH CHANAN 12, 13

48 Whoever rejects me and takes not my word
         has one who judges him:
   the word I word judges him in the final day.

49   For I word not of my own soul;
   but the Father who apostolized me gave me a misvah
         — what to word*, and what to word*:
   *a play on two different words with almost the same meaning
50 and I know his misvah is life/salvation eternal:
              so whatever I word
         as the Father words to me, thus I word.

The Final Night of Yah Shua: the Final Supper

13:1 And preceding the feast of the pasach,
         Yah Shua, knowing his hour arrived
         to depart from this cosmos to the Father,
         loving his own who are in the cosmos,
              he loves them to the finality.

Yah Shua Purifies the Feet of the Disciples

2   And being supper;
           Satan places into the heart
   of Yah Hudah the urbanite the son of Shimon
              to shalam him.

3   And Yah Shua,
           because of knowing
   all that the Father gave into his hands
   and that he comes from God and goes to God,
4 he rises from supper and places his garment;
     and takes a linen and girds his loins;
5   and places water into a washbasin
   and begins to wash the feet of the disciples;
   and to wipe them with the linen he girt his loins.

6   And when he comes to Shimon Kepha:
           Shimon words to him,
           My Lord, you — wash my feet?

7   Yah Shua answers, wording to him,
           What I work you know not now;
              and afterwards you know.

8   Shimon Kepha words to him,
           You wash not my feet eternally.

           Yah Shua words to him,
   If I wash you not, you have no part with me.

9   Shimon Kepha words to him,
           My Lord, wash not only my feet
           but also my hands and also my head.

10   Yah Shua words to him,
           Whoever is washed, need not wash
           — only his feet, for he is all pure.

           Also you are all pure — but not all.
11   — for Yah Shua knows who is to shalam him;
   because of this, he words, You are not all pure.

Foot Purifying Example

12   And when he washes their feet,
           takes his garment and reposes,
              and words to them,
           Know you what I worked to you?
13   You call to me, Rabbi and Lord:
           and you word well; for I am.
14 So if I, your Lord and Rabbi, wash your feet;
              how much more
   you are indebted to wash the feet of one by one:

15   for I give you this example
         to also work as I work to you.

16   Amen! Amen! I word to you,
              Neither is the servant
              greater than his Lord;
              nor the apostolized
         greater than he who apostolized him.
17   Whenever you know these,
         graced — whenever you work them.

18   I word not concerning you all:
           for I know whom I selected:
           but to shalam the Scripture,
           He who eats bread with me
         exalts concerning his heel against me.
                              Psalm 41:9

19   Now I word to you ere it becomes,
   so, whenever it becomes, you trust that I — I.

20   Amen! Amen! I word to you,
   Whoever takes whomever I apostolize, takes me;
              and whoever takes me,
              takes him who apostolized me.

21   Wording this, Yah Shua sighs in spirit,
              and witnesses, and words,
              Amen! Amen! I word to you,
              that one of you shalams me.

22   And the disciples look one to one,
   because of not knowing concerning whom he words:
23   and one of his disciples
           reposing in the bosom of Yah Shua
           whom Yah Shua befriends*:
                        see: Yah Chanan 21:20
24   Shimon Kepha signs
   to ask him concerning whom he words.

25   Then the disciple,
         falling on the chest of Yah Shua,
   and words to him, My Lord, who is this?

26   Yah Shua answers, wording,
   He to whom I give a bread when I immerse it.
              — and he immerses the bread
         and gives it to Yah Hudah the urbanite
              the son of Shimon.

Satan Enters Yah Hudah

27 And after the bread, then Satan enters in him:
           and Yah Shua words to him,
           What you work, work quickly.

28   And of those reposing,
   no human knows concerning whom he words
29   For some humans hope,
         because of Yah Hudah having the bag,
         that in misvahing, he was misvahed,
   Merchandise what we seek for the the feast;
         or, Give somewhat to the poor.

30   And Yah Hudah takes the bread
           and straightway goes outside:
           and being night when he goes.

31   Yah Shua words,
         Now the Son of humanity glorifies;
         and whenever God glorifies in him,
           God also glorifies him in himself,
              and straightway glorifies him.

YAH CHANAN 13, 14

33 My sons,
another little I am with you.
You seek me:
and as I word to the Yah Hudiym,
Where I go, you are not able to come;
— I also word now to you.

A NEW MISVAH

34 A new misvah I give you
— of loving one to one;
as I love you, you also love one to one:
35 by this all humanity knows you are my disciples
— whenever loving one to one.

36 Shimon Kepha words to him,
Our Lord, where go you?

Yah Shua answers, wording to him,
Where I go, you are not now able to come after me
— and finally you come.

37 Shimon Kepha words to him,
My Lord, why am I not able to come after you now?
I place my soul in your stead.

38 Yah Shua words to him,
You, place your soul in my stead?
Amen! Amen! I word to you,
The rooster calls not,
until you deny me three times.

YAH SHUA PROMISES HIS PAROUSIA

14:1 Trouble not your heart:
trust in God; trust also in me.
2 In the house of my Father are many abodes:
and if not, I had worded to you.
I go preparing a place for you:
3 and whenever I go preparing a place for you
I come again and guide you unto myself;
that where I be, you also be.
4 And where I go you know, and the way you know.

5 Taoma words to him,
Our Lord, we know not where you go;
and how are we able to know the way?

6 Yah Shua words to him,
I — I the way, the truth, and the life/salvation:
humanity comes not to the Father, but by me.
7 If you had known me,
you had also known my Father:
and from now you know him and you see him.

8 Philipaus words to him,
Our Lord, show us the Father, and it suffices us.

9 Yah Shua words to him,
Have I been evermore with you,
and you know me not, Philipaus?
Whoever sees me sees the Father!
And how word you, Show us the Father?
10 Trust you not, I in my Father,
and my Father in me?
The word I word to you,
I word not from my own soul:
and the Father inhabiting in me works these works.

11 Trust — I in my Father,
and my Father in me:
if not, trust even because of the works.

12 Amen! Amen! I word to you,
Whoever trusts in me,
also works the works I work:
— and works more than these
because I go to my Father.

13 And whatever you ask in my name, I work,
to glorify the Father in the Son.
14 And whenever you ask in my name, I work.
15 Whenever you befriend me, guard my misvoth.

YAH SHUA PROMISES THE PARACLETE

16 I seek of the Father;
and he gives you another Paraclete
to be with you eternally
17 — the Spirit of truth;
whom the cosmos is not able to take
because it neither sees him, nor knows him:
and you know him;
for he inhabits you, being in you.

18 I forsake you not orphaned;
for in a little I come to you:
19 and the cosmos sees me not;
but you see me:
because I live, you enliven.
20 In that day you know,
I in my Father, and you in me, and I in you.

21 Whoever has my misvoth and guards them
loves me:
and whoever befriends me
is befriended by my Father;
and I befriend him and show my own soul to him.

22 Yah Hudah words to him — not the urbanite,
My Lord,
why prepare you to show your own soul to us,
and not to the cosmos?

23 Yah Shua answers, wording to him,
whenever anyone befriends me, he guards my words;
and my Father befriends him:
and we come to him and work our abode with him.

24 Whoever befriends me not, guards not my words:
and this word you have heard is not my own
but of the Father who apostolized me.
25 I word these to you, being with you.

26 And the Paraclete — the Holy Spirit
whom the Father apostolizes in my name,
he doctrinates all;
and reminds you of all I word to you.

YAH SHUA BESTOWS HIS UNITY

27 I allow shalom with you;
my own shalom I give to you:
not as the cosmos gives, give I you:
neither trouble your heart; nor awe.

28 You heard me word to you, I go, and come to you.

If you befriend me,
cheer that I go to the Father:
for my Father is greater than I.

29 And now, behold, I word to you, ere it becomes,
that, whatever becomes, you trust.

30 So I word not much with you:
for the arch of this cosmos comes,
not having aught in me.
31 But so that the cosmos knows
that I befriend the Father,
and as the Father misvahed me,
likewise I work.

Rise, we go hence.

ABIDING IN THE VINE

15:1 I — I the vine of truth,
and my Father the cultivator.
2 Every branch in me not giving fruit he takes away:
and all giving fruit, he purifies to bring much fruit.
3 You already — you are pure
because of the word I worded with you.

4 Abide in me, and I in you.
As the branch
is not able to give fruit from its own soul
if not it abide in the vine;
thus not even you
if not you abide in me.
5 I — I the vine and you the branches:
whoever abides in me, and I in him,
this brings much fruit:
because without me you are not able to work aught.

6 If not humanity abides in me,
he is cast outside as a branch that withered;
and they gather them
and cast them into the fire to burn.
7 And whenever you abide in me,
and my word abides in you
ask all you will, and it becomes to you.
8 Herein is my Father glorified
— that you bring much fruit;
and be my disciples.
9 As the Father loves me, I also love you:
abide in my friendship.

10 Whenever you guard my misvoth,
you abide in my love;
as I guard the misvoth of my Father,
and abide in his love.

11 I word these with you,
so that my cheer be in you,
and to fulfill your cheer.

12 This is my misvah:
to love one to one, as I love you.

13 Greater love has no one than this,
than for humanity
to place his soul in the stead of his friends:
14 you are my friends,
whenever you work all I misvah you.

THE NEW RELATIONSHIP

15 Now I call you not, servants;
because the servant knows not what his Lord works:
and I call you, my friends;
because all I heard from my Father, I notified you.

16 You selected me not, but I selected you,
and placed you to go and bring fruit,
and that your fruit abide:
that all you ask of the Father in my name,
he gives you.

17 This I misvah you: to love one to one.
18 Whenever the cosmos hates you,
you know it hated me ere you.
19 And if you be of the cosmos,
the cosmos ever befriends his own:
but you be not of the cosmos,
for I selected you from the cosmos:
because of this the cosmos hates you.

20 Remember the word I worded to you,
The servant be not greater than his Lord.
Whenever they persecute me,
they also persecute you:
whenever they guard my word,
they also guard yours.
21 But they work all these to you
because of my name,
because they know not him who apostolized me.

22 If I had not come and worded with them,
they had not had sin:
and now they have no pretext concerning their sin.

23 Whoever hates me also hates my Father.
24 If I had not worked the work in their eyes
which no other human worked,
they had not had sin:
and now they have seen and have hated
even me and even my Father
25 — to fulfill the word scribed in their torah,
They hated me freely.

Psalms 35:19, 61:4

26 And whenever the Paraclete comes
— whom I apostolize to you from the Father
— even the Spirit of truth
who proceeds from the Father,
27 you also witness,
— you were with me from the beginning.

EJECTION AND MARTYRDOM

16:1 I word this with you,
that you not be offended.
2 For they eject you from the congregation:
and the hour comes that all who slaughter you
think they offer God qurbana:
3 and they work these to you
because they know neither the Father, nor me:
4 I word these with you,
that whatever the season brings,
you remember that I told you of them.
And I worded these not to you from formerly.

5 And now I go my way to him who apostolized me;
and humanity asks me not, Where go you?
6 For I word these to you,
and sorrow fills your heart.

THE MINISTRY OF THE PARACLETE

7 But I word the truth to you;
It is beneficial for you that I go:
for if ever I go not,
the Paraclete comes not to you:
and whenever I depart, I apostolize him to you:

YAH CHANAN 16, 17

8 and when he comes,
he rebukes the cosmos
concerning sin,
and concerning justness,
and concerning judgment.

9 Concerning sin,
because they trust not in me;
10 and concerning justness,
because I go to my Father,
and you see me not again;
11 and concerning judgment,
because the arch of this cosmos is judged.

12 Again, I have much to word to you,
but you are not able to hold them now.

13 And when the Spirit of truth comes,
he guides you into all truth:
for he words not from his own soul;
but all he hears, he words,
and he prepares you and notifies you.

14 He glorifies me:
because he takes from my own, and shows to you.

YAH SHUA PROPHESIES HIS DEATH, RESURRECTION, AND PAROUSIA

15 All my Father has is mine.
Because of this, I word to you,
He takes of my own, and shows you.

16 A little, and you see me not;
and again, A little, and you see me;
— I go to the Father.

17 And some of his disciples word one to one,
What is this that he words to us,
A little, and you see me not:
and again, A little, and you see me:
and, I go to the Father?

18 And they word,
What is this that he words, A little?
We know not what he words.

19 And Yah Shua knows that they seek to ask him,
and he words to them concerning this,
Seek you with one another concerning what I word,
A little, and you see me not:
and again, A little, and you see me?

20 Amen! Amen! I word to you,
You weep and mourn, and the cosmos cheers:
and you sorrow, but your sorrow becomes cheer.

21 A woman, whenever she births, sorrows,
because her day of birthing arrives:
and whenever she births the son,
she remembers not the travail,
because of the cheer
that a son of humanity is birthed into the cosmos.

22 Now also, you sorrow:
and I see you again, and cheer your heart,
and humanity takes not your cheer from you:
23 and in that day you ask me not aught.

Amen! Amen! I word to you,
All that you ask the Father in my name,
he gives you.

24 Until now, you asked not aught in my name:
ask and take to fulfill your cheer.

25 I word these to you with parables:
and the hour comes,
when I word not to you with parables,
but I show you openly concerning the Father.
26 In that day you ask in my name:
and I word not to you,
that I ask of the Father concerning you:
27 for the Father befriends you,
because you befriend me,
and trust that I come from God.

28 I came from the Father and came into the cosmos.
Again, I forsake the cosmos, and go to the Father.

29 His disciples word to him,
Behold, now you word openly, and word no parable:
30 now we know that you know all,
and need not humanity to ask you:
in this we trust — that you came from God.

31 Yah Shua answers them, Trust.
32 Behold, the hour comes — now comes,
that you disperse — humanity to his place,
and forsake me alone:
and I be not alone — the father is with me.

33 I word these to you
that in me you have shalom.
In the cosmos you have tribulation:
but, courage! I triumph over the cosmos.

THE PRAYER OF YAH SHUA TO THE FATHER

17:1 Yah Shua words these
and lifts his eyes to the heavens, and words,
My Father, the hour is come; glorify your Son,
so that your Son glorifies you:
2 as you gave him sultanship concerning all flesh
to give eternal life/salvation to all you give him.
3 And this is eternal life/salvation:
that they know you the only God of truth,
and Yah Shua Meshiach whom you apostolized.
4 I glorified you on the earth:
I shalamed the work you gave me to work.

5 And now glorify me, O Father, with you,
with the glory I had being with you
from ere the cosmos be.

6 I notified your name to the sons of humanity
whom you gave me from eternity:
being your own, and giving them to me;
and they guarded your word.

7 Now they know that all — whatever you gave me
are from you:
8 for I gave them the word you gave to me;
and they have taken;
and know truly that I come from you;
and they trust that you apostolized me.

9 I seek concerning them:
I seek not concerning the cosmos,
but concerning those you gave to me;
for they are yours:
10 and all my own are yours,
and your own are mine;
and I am glorified in them.

Yah Chanan 17, 18

11 And now not being in the cosmos,
and these being in the cosmos,
I come to you, Holy Father:
guard in your own name those whom you gave to me,
that they be one, as we.

12 When being with them in the cosmos
guarding them in your name;
whom you gave me, I guarded:
and of these humans, none destructs
but the son of destruction.

13 And now I come to you;
and I word these in the cosmos
to fulfill my cheer in them.
14 I gave them your word;
and the cosmos hates them
not being of the cosmos
— as I be not of the cosmos.

15 I seek you not to take them from the cosmos,
but to guard them from vilifying
16 — not being of the cosmos
as I be not of the cosmos.
17 Father, hallow them in your truth:
your own word is truth.

18 As you apostolized me into the cosmos,
I also send them into the cosmos.

19 And concerning them I hallow my own soul,
that they also be hallowed in the truth.

The Prayer of Yah Shua for Future Trusters

20 And I seek not concerning these only,
but also concerning them
who trust in me through their word;
21 that they all be one;
as you, my Father in me; and I in you;
that they also be one in us:
that the cosmos trust that you sent me.

22 And the glory you gave me, I gave to them;
being one — one as we:
23 I in them, and you in me,
being perfected in one;
and that the cosmos know that you apostolized me,
and loved them as you also loved me.

24 Father, those whom you gave to me
I will also to be with me;
— seeing my own glory that you gave me:
for you loved me
from ere the foundation of the cosmos.

25 O just Father,
the cosmos knows you not; and I know you:
and these know that you apostolized me:
26 and I notified your name to them;
and notify
that the love with which you love me be in them;
and I in them.

Yah Shua in the Garden

18:1 Yah Shua words these,
and goes with his disciples
crossing the brook Qidron where there be a garden,
where he and his disciples enter:
2 and Yah Hudah the shalamer also knows the place:
because of Yah Shua often congregating there
with his disciples.

Yah Hudah Shalams Yah Shua

3 So Yah Hudah guides a squad
and of the Rabbipriests and Pharisiym,
and guides the guards;
and comes there
with lanterns and lamps and armor.

4 And Yah Shua,
knowing all that comes concerning him,
goes and words to them, Whom seek you?

5 They answer him, Yah Shua the Nazrayaim.

Yah Shua words to them, I — I.
And Yah Hudah also rises
— the shalamer with them.

6 And when Yah Shua words to them, I — I,
they go backward, and fall on the earth.

7 Again Yah Shua asks them, Whom seek you?

And they word, Yah Shua the Nazrayaim.

8 Yah Shua answers, I word to you, I — I:
and if you seek me, release these to go.
9 — to shalam the word he had worded,
Of whom you gave me, not one of them destruct.

10 And Shimon Kepha, having a sword,
draws and strikes the servant of the Rabbipriest,
and takes his right ear.
— the name of the servant, Malech.

11 And Yah Shua words to Kepha,
Place your sword into the sheath:
the cup my Father gives to me, drink I not?

Yah Shua Arrested

12 Then the squad and the chiliarch
and guards of the Yah Hudiym
hold Yah Shua, and bind him;
13 and lead him away to Hanan first;
— because of being father in law to Qauapha,
having been the Rabbipriest that same year
14 — the Qauapha
who had counseled the Yah Hudiym
that it is beneficial
that one man die in the stead of the people.

The First Denial of Petros

15 And Shimon Kepha and one of the other disciples
come after Yah Shua:
and that disciple knowing the Rabbipriest;
enters with Yah Shua into the dwelling.

16 And Kepha standing outside at the portal:
and that other disciple,
knowing the Rabbipriest,
words to the guard of the portal to bring Shimon in.

17 And the lass — the guard of the portal
words to Kepha,
Are not you also of the disciples of this man?

He words, Not.

18 And standing there,
the servants and attendants set a fire to warm,
because of being cold:
and Shimon standing with them, and warming.

YAH CHANAN 18, 19

THE WITNESS OF YAH SHUA

19 And the Rabbipriest asks Yah Shua
concerning his disciples and concerning his doctrine.

20 Yah Shua words to him,
I worded openly with the people;
I ever doctrinated in the congregation
and in the priestal precinct
where all the Yah Hudiym congregate;
and I worded not aught in secret.

21 Why ask me?
Ask them who heard me word with them:
behold, they know all that I worded.

22 And when he words these,
one of the guards rises
striking Yah Shua on the cheek,
wording, Give you word to the Rabbipriest thus?

23 Yah Shua answers, wording to him,
If I have worded evilly,
witness concerning the villifying:
and if well, why strike me?

24 And Hanan apostolizes to bind Yah Shua
to Qauapha the Rabbipriest.

THE SECOND DENIAL OF PETROS

25 And Shimon Kepha, rising and warming himself:
and they are wording to him,
Why? Are not you also one of his disciples?

And denying he words, Not I.

THE THIRD DENIAL OF PETROS

26 One of the servants of the Rabbipriest,
being kin of him whose ear Shimon cut,
words, Saw I not you in the garden with him?

27 And again Shimon denies:
— and in that hour the rooster calls.

THE TRIAL OF YAH SHUA

28 And they bring Yah Shua
from Qauapha to the praetorium:
having been dawn;
and they enter not the praetorium,
that they soil not while eating the pasach.

29 And Pilataus goes to them, and words to them,
What accusation have you concerning this man?

30 They answer, and word to him,
If he were not a worker of evil,
we had not shalamed him to you.

31 Pilataus words to them,
You guide him and judge him as to your torah.

The Yah Hudiym word to him,
We are not allowed to slaughter humanity:
32 — to shalam the word Yah Shua worded
notifying by which death he is prepared to die.

33 And Pilataus enters the praetorium again,
and calls to Yah Shua, and words to him,
Are you the Sovereign of the Yah Hudiym?

34 Yah Shua words to him,
Word you this of your own soul?
Or word others to you concerning me?

35 Pilataus words, Why? I — a Yah Hudiy?
Your own people and the Rabbipriests
shalamed you to me.
What worked you?

36 Yah Shua words,
My own sovereigndom be not of this cosmos:
if my sovereigndom be of this cosmos,
my ministers had striven
that I not be shalamed to the Yah Hudiym:
and now my sovereigndom be not from here.

37 Pilataus words to him,
Then are you a sovereign?

Yah Shua words to him,
You word that I — I a sovereign.
For this I was birthed,
and for this I came into the cosmos
— to witness concerning the truth.
Whoever is of the truth hears my voice.

38 Pilataus words to him, What is truth?
— and when he words this
he goes again to the Yah Hudiym, and words to them,
I am not able to find in him any pretext:
39 and you have a custom,
that I release one to you at the pasach:
so will you that I release to you
this Sovereign of the Yah Hudiym?

YAH HUDIYM DEMAND YAH SHUA

40 And again they all shout, wording,
Not this — but Bar Aba.
— and this Bar Aba has been a robber.

YAH SHUA WREATHED

19:1 Then Pilataus scourges Yah Shua:
2 and the strategists braid a wreath of thorns
and place it on his head;
and they cover him in a garment of purple;
3 and word, Shalom!
Sovereign of the Yah Hudiym!
— and they strike him on the cheek.

4 Pilataus goes outside again and words to them,
Behold, I bring him outside to you,
to notify you that I am not able
to find even one pretext against him.

5 And Yah Shua goes outside
having the wreath of thorns
and the garment of purple:
and Pilataus words to them, Behold the man!

6 And when the Rabbipriests and guards see him
they shout, wording, Stake! Stake!

Pilataus words to them, You guide him, and stake:
for I am not able to find any pretext in him.

7 The Yah Hudiym word to him,
We have a torah,
and by our torah he is indebted to die
because he works his own soul, the Son of God.

8 And when Pilataus hears this word
he is excessively awestricken;
9 and again enters the praetorium,
and words to Yah Shua, Whence are you?
— and Yah Shua gives no answer to him.

YAH CHANAN 19

10 Pilataus words to him, Word you not with me?
Know you not that I am allowed to release you,
and I am allowed to stake you?

11 Yah Shua words,
You have no sultanship at all concerning me,
— not even one
if not given you from above:
because of this, whoever shalams me to you
his sin is greater than your own.
12 And because of this, Pilataus wills to release him:
and the Yah Hudiym shout, wording,
If ever you release this one,
you are no friend of the kaisar:
for all who works his own soul a sovereign
is contrary to the kaisar.

13 And when Pilataus hears this word,
he brings Yah Shua outside,
and sits on the bamah
— in a place called the Pavement of Stone;
and Hebraically, worded, Gepipta.

14 And being the eve of the pasach,
and having been as the hour of six:
and he words to the Yah Hudiym,
Behold your sovereign!

15 And they shout, Take! Take! Stake! Stake!

Pilataus words to them, Stake your Sovereign?

The Rabbipriests word to him,
We have no sovereign but the kaisar.

YAH SHUA STAKED

16 Then he shalams him to them to stake:
and they guide Yah Shua, and eject him;
17 while bearing his stake to a place
called, Cranium,
and Hebraically, worded, Gagulta:
18 where they stake him — with two others
— one hence and one hence
and Yah Shua midst.

19 And Pilataus also scribes a tablet,
and places it on the stake:
and the scribing is thus:
This is Yah Shua the Nazrayaim
Sovereign of the Yah Hudim.

20 And many of the Yah Hudiym call this board:
because the place they stake Yah Shua
is near the city:
and being scribed
in Hebraic and Hellenic and Romaic.

21 And the Rabbipriests word to Pilataus,
Scribe not, The Sovereign of the Yah Hudiym;
but, He words I am Sovereign of the Yah Hudiym.

22 Pilataus words, What I scribed I scribed.

WARRIORS GAMBLE OVER THE GARMENTS OF YAH SHUA

23 And the strategists, when they stake Yah Shua,
they take his garment, and make four parts
— one part to each strategist:
and the tunic being not threaded,
all woven from on the top.

24 And they word one to one,
Tear not, but toss and toss for it, whose it becomes:
— to shalam the Scripture, wording,
They divided my garment among them;
and on my garments they cast lots.
— these the strategists worked.
Psalm 22:18

YAH SHUA PRESENTS HIS MOTHER TO YAH CHANAN

25 And standing toward the stake of Yah Shua
are his mother,
and the sister of his mother, Maryam of Qeleyaupa,
and Maryam the Magdelauta.

26 And Yah Shua, seeing his mother,
— and the disciple whom he befriends, standing,
he words to his mother, Woman, behold your son!
27 then he words to the disciple, Behold your mother!
— and from that hour
that disciple guides her to his own.

YAH SHUA THIRSTS

28 After this, Yah Shua,
knowing that all are shalamed
— to fulfill the Scripture, words, I thirst.
29 — and they place a vessel full of vinegar:
and fill a sponge of vinegar and put it on hyssop
and offer it to his mouth.

30 And when he takes the vinegar,
Yah Shua words, Behold, Shalamed:
and he bows his head and shalams his spirit.

PROPHESIES FULFILLED

31 And the Yah Hudiym, because of being the eve,
word that the flesh not remain on the stake
because the Shabbath dawns
— for this day being a great Shabbath:
and they seek Pilataus
to break the shins of those staked
and descend them.

32 And the strategists come,
and break the shin of the first
and of the other staked with him:
33 and when they come to Yah Shua
and see that he already died,
they break not his shins:
34 but one of the strategists
strikes his side with a spear,
and straightway blood and water eject.

35 And he who sees, witnesses;
and his witness is true: .
and he knows that he words truth, that you also trust.

36 For these became to fulfill the Scripture,
wording, No bone of him breaks.

37 And again another Scripture words,
They look at him whom they pierce.
Psalm 34:20, Zechar Yah 12:10

THE BODY OF YAH SHUA TAKEN

38 After these,
Yauseph of Ramtak, seeks of Pilataus,
because of being a disciple of Yah Shua,
and secreting himself for awe of the Yah Hudiym,
to take the flesh of Yah Shua
— and Pilataus allows him.
And he comes, and takes the flesh of Yah Shua:

YAH CHANAN 19, 20

39   and Niqadimus also comes
— who formerly came to Yah Shua by night
and bringing a spicery of myrrh and aloes
— as one hundred litra.

40   And they take the flesh of Yah Shua
and bind it in linen with the ointment,
as the custom of the Yah Hudiym to entomb.

Yah Shua Entombed

41   And there in the place Yah Shua was staked;
is a garden:
and in the garden
a new house of a tomb
wherein no human had ever been placed:
42   and there they place Yah Shua
because of the Shabbath beginning;
and because of the tomb being near.

Yah Shua Disentombed

20:1   And on a first Shabbath
Maryam the Magdelauta
comes at dawn while dark
to the house of the tomb,
and sees the stone taken from the tomb.
2   And she runs and comes to Shimon Kepha
and to the other disciple whom Yah Shua befriends
and words to them,
They took our Lord from the house of the tomb,
and we know not where they placed him.

3   And Kepha and that other disciple go
and come to the house of the tomb
4   — and they run — the two being in union:
and the other disciple runs preceding Shimon,
and comes to the house of the tomb first:
5   and he looks and sees the linen placed;
and he enters not.

6   And Shimon comes after him
and enters the house of the tomb;
and sees the linen placed:
7   and the sudarium
which had been girt around his head
not lying with the linen
but bound and placed alongside one place.

8   Then that disciple also enters
— who had come to the house of the tomb first:
and he sees and trusts.
9   — for as yet not knowing of the Scripture
that he prepares rising from the dead.
10   — and the disciples go again to their place.

The Resurrected Yah Shua Appears to Maryam

11   And Maryam, standing by the tomb weeping,
and while weeping, she looks into the tomb,
12   and sees two angels in white seated;
one by the pillow and one by the feet,
where the flesh of Yah Shua be placed.

13   And they word to her, Woman, why weep you?

              She words to them,
Because they took my Lord
and I know not where they placed him.
14   — she words thus,
and turns back and sees Yah Shua standing;
and not knowing it be Yah Shua.

15   Yah Shua words to her,
Woman, why weep you? Whom seek you?

       And she, hoping him to be the gardener,
words to him,
My lord, if you took him,
word to me where you placed him, and I take him.

16   Yah Shua words to her, Maryam.

       She turns, and words to him Hebraically, Rabuli!
— which is to word, Doctor.

17   Yah Shua words to her, Approach me not;
for I have not yet ascended to my Father:
and go to my brothers, and word to them,
I ascend to my Father, and your Father;
and my God, and your God.

18   Then Maryam the Magdelauta comes
and evangelizes the disciples that she saw our Lord
and that he worded these to her.

The Resurrected Yah Shua Appears to Ten Disciples

19   And when it became the evening of the day,
being a first shabbath,
the portals being shut where the disciples assemble
because of awe of the Yah Hudiym,
Yah Shua comes and stands among them,
and words to them, Shalom with you.

20   He words this,
and shows them his hands and his side;
and the disciples cheer when they see the Lord.

21   And Yah Shua words to them again,
Shalom with you:
as my Father apostolized me,
I also apostolize you.

The Resurrected Yah Shua Bestows the Holy Spirit

22   And when he words this,
he puffs into them and words to them,
Take the Holy Spirit:
23   whenever you forgive the sins of humanity,
they are forgiven to them;
and whenever you hold of humanity,
they are held.

Taoma Appears

24   And Taoma, one of the twelve, worded Twin,
not being there with them when Yah Shua came:
25   and the disciples word to him,
We saw our Lord.

            And he words to them,
If not I see in his hands the place of the nails,
and place my finger in them,
and extend my hand into his side,
I trust not.

The Resurrected Yah Shua Appears to Eleven Disciples

26   And again after eight days
his disciples being inside
and Taoma with them:
Yah Shua comes, when the portals are held,
and stands midst them, and words,
Shalom with you.

YAH CHANAN 20, 21

27 — and he words to Taoma,
Bring here your finger and see my hands;
and bring your hand and extend into my side:
and be not not trusting, but trusting.

THE WITNESS OF TAOMA TO THE DEITY OF YAH SHUA

28 And Taoma answers him, wording to him,
My Lord and my God.

29 Yah Shua words to him,
Taoma, now that you see me, you trust:
graced — whoever see not and trusts.

30 And Yah Shua works many other signs
in front of his disciples,
which are not scribed in this Scripture:
31 and these are also scribed so that you trust
that Yah Shua is the Meshiach the Son of God;
and that trusting in his name
you have eternal life/salvation.

THE RESURRECTED YAH SHUA MANIFESTS HIMSELF AGAIN

21:1 After these
Yah Shua again shows his own soul
to his disciples on the sea of Tiberiyaus;
and he shows himself thus:
2 there being, in union,
Shimon Kepha and Taoma — worded Twin
and Nathan El from Qanah of Galiyl
and the sons of Zabedai
and two of his other disciples.

3 Shimon Kepha words to them,
I go catch fish.

They word to him, We also come with you.
— and they go and ascend into a sailer;
and that night they catch not aught.

CASTING THE NET

4 And being dawn,
Yah Shua stands on the hand of the sea:
and the disciples know not he be Yah Shua:
5 and Yah Shua words to them,
Lads, have you somewhat to eat?

They word to him, Not.

6 And he words to them,
Cast the net from the right side of the sailer,
and you are able.

And they cast;
and are not able to draw the net
of the multitude of fishes held.

7 And that disciple whom Yah Shua befriends
words to Kepha, This is our Lord.

And when Shimon hears it is our Lord,
he takes his linen and girds his loins
— because of being naked:
and he casts his soul into the sea
to come to Yah Shua
8 — and the other disciples come in a sailer
— for not being very far from earth
but as two hundred cubits
drawing the net with fishes:

9 and when they ascend to earth,
they see a fire of live coals
and fish placed about and bread.
10 And Yah Shua words to them,
Bring of the fish you now caught.

11 Shimon Kepha ascends
and draws the net full of great fishes to earth
— a hundred and fifty—three
and with all this weight, the net splits not.

12 Yah Shua words to them, Come, dine.
And not a human of the disciples dare ask him
who he be
— knowing it is the Lord.

13 And Yah Shua approaches and takes the bread
and the fish
and gives to them.

14 This is time three
Yah Shua is seen by his disciples
after rising from the house of the dead.

LOVE VS BEFRIEND

15 And when they dine,
Yah Shua words to Shimon Kepha,
Shimon son of Yonah,
love you me much more than these?

He words to him, Yes, My Lord;
you know I befriend you.

He words to him, Feed my lambs.

16 He words to him again time two,
Shimon, son of Yonah love you me?

He words to him, Yes, my Lord;
you know I befriend you.

He words to him, Shepherd my sheep.

17 He words to him time three,
Shimon, son of Yonah, befriend you me?

And Kepha sorrows
because he words to him time three,
Befriend you me?

And he words to him, My Lord, you are enwisened:
you — you know I befriend you.

Yah Shua words to him, Shepherd my sheep.

YAH SHUA PROPHESIES THE MARTYRDOM OF PETROS

18 Amen! Amen! I word to you,
When being a lad,
you, by your own soul, binding your loins
and walking where you willed:
and whenever you senesce
you extend your hands;
and another binds your loins for you,
and bears you where you will not.
19 — and He words this
to show by what death he prepares to glorify God:
— and when he words this,
he words to him, Come after me.

YAH CHANAN 21

20 And Shimon Kepha turns
and sees the disciple Yah Shua befriends,
who had come after him
— who, had fallen at supper
on the chest of Yah Shua
and had worded, My Lord, who shalams you?
Yah Chanan 13:21—25

21 When he sees him, Kepha words to Yah Shua,
My Lord, and this — what?

22 Yah Shua words to him,
If ever I will him to abide until I come,
what — to you?
You, come after me.

23 And this word goes among the brothers,
that that disciple dies not:
And Yah Shua worded not, He dies not;
but, If ever I will him to abide until I come,
what — to you?

CONCLUSION

24 This is the disciple
who witnesses concerning all these
and also scribes these:
and we know his witness is true.

25 And there are also many others
Yah Shua worked
which, if they be scribed one by one,
not even the cosmos,
as I hope,
is able for the Scripture being scribed.

Amen

YAH CHANAN   CONCISE DEFINITIONS

KEY:
The first word in **bold** is the word under consideration:
The second word in plain text is the Aramaic:
The words in *italic* indicate the part of speech:
The words following are the definition.

amen amen *transliterated adverb, noun, verb* one of two words which is identical in every langauge. It is the root of the adverb, noun, and verb, trust (believe, faith).
apostle seliba *noun title* one having been commissioned.
apostolize sadar *verb* to commission.
bamah bamah *transliterated noun* seat of judgment.
be, become, being hewa *noun, participle, verb* the state of existing, or coming into existence.
congregate kenas *verb* to gather.
congregation kensa *noun* a gathering.
destroy ebad *verb* to demolish.
destruction abdana *noun* demolition.
doctor malpana *noun* one who doctrinates.
doctrinate yilep *verb* to teach.
eternal alma *adjective* of infinate duration.
eulogize berek *verb* to bless, to praise.
eulogy burketa *noun* a blessing, a praise.
exalt ram *verb* to lift.
grotto mearta *noun* cave.
guard metarta, natura, neturta *noun, participle* a protector.
God El, Alaha *proper noun* Diety.
guard netar *verb* to observe, to protect, to regard.
having been it hewa *two verbs* when occurring together, these two words indicate a state of continuing existence.
Hoshia Na usana *noun* Save us now: from the prophecy of Psalm 118:25, to the fulfillment in Yah Chanan 12:12,13.
human, humanity nasa *noun* the species created by God on day six to dominate over the rest of his creation.
I — I ena — ena *double pronoun* the Aramaic equivelant of the Hebraic I AM — the eternal deity.
life/salvation haye *noun* this one word has a two—fold meaning.
lord mare *title* one having authority over another, whether in ownership over a slave or property, in partnership with a lady, or a position in politics.
Maryam Maryam *proper name* quite possibly the feminine of lord.
merchandise tegurta *noun* that being bought or sold.
merchandise zeban *verb* to buy and/or sell.
merchant tagura *noun, title* one who buys and sells.
Meshiach mesiha *title* anointed one.
misvah puqdana *noun* a command.
misvah peqad *verb* to command.
nave haikla *noun* the holy of holies: compare priestal precinct.
notify yida *verb* to make known.
pasach pesha *noun* a feast of the Yah Hudim.
priestal precinct haikla *noun* the holies: compare nave. NOTE: the Aramaic does not distinguish between the nave and the priestal precinct as do the Habraic and Hellenic.
qurbana qurbana *noun* a hallowed oblation.
Rabbi Rabi *title* Great One in the Rabbinical hierarchy.
Rabbipriest Rab Kahna *title* Great Priest.
Rabuli Rabuli *transliterated title* Rabbi.
raise qam *verb* to erect, to cause to rise,.to stand.
raze setar *verb* to demolish, to lay level with the earth.
Shabbath Sabeta *noun* the seventh day of the week: a day of hallowed festivities.
shalam shelem *transliterated verb* the verb of shalom: to satisfy fully, to fully satisfy — whether of being in a state of contentment and/or peace, or fully satisfying an obligation, or even the sense of getting even by betraying.
shalamer mashlemana *participle* one who fully satisifes self in the sense of getting even by betraying.
shalom selema *noun* the state of being fully satisfied or satisfied fully — whether in a state of contentment and/or peace.
sign ata *noun* a signification: a work worked, usually to indicate the diety of the worker: often mistranslated, miracle.
sign remaz *verb* to communicate by signing and/or signaling.
son of humanity bar nasa *compound noun* see human, humanity.
sovereign malka *title* one who is above all others — whether Kaisers, Kings, Pharohs, Sultans, or whomever.
sultan, sultanship sultana *title* one in authority: the position of authority.
tomb qabra *noun* a house of the dead.
will sebyana *noun* the mental and spiritual attribute including, but not limited to, memory, volition.
will seba *verb* that action stemming from the mental and spiritual attribute.
word melta *noun* word, in Scripture, is more than the vocalization of a thought; word includes, but is not limited to a promise: Yah Shua Meshiach is the Word of God.
word emar *verb* in Scripture, is more than vocalizing a thought: word includes, but is not limited to, promising or giving one's word.
Yah Chanan *proper noun* beloved of Yah.
Yah Shua Yesu *proper name* Eternal Salvation: the name of our Lord and Meshiach.
— ing *suffix* In this translation, —ing is added to verbs preceding or following the verbs have or be, to indicate eternal or continuing action.